THE SEVENTH AND REVISED POPULAR EDITION.

AN

ILLUSTRATED TREATISE

ON

THE ART OF SHOOTING,

WITH EXTRACTS FROM THE

BEST AUTHORITIES.

(90 ILLUSTRATIONS.)

BY

CHARLES LANCASTER,

GUN, RIFLE AND PISTOL MANUFACTURER

BY WARRANTS OF APPOINTMENT TO

H. M. The King, H. I. M. The German Emperor, H. R. H. Prince Christian,
H. I. H. The Grand Duke Vladimir, H. R. H. The Duke of Orleans, &c., &c.

(Established in 1826 at 151, New Bond Street, London, W.)

REMOVED TO

11, PANTON STREET, HAYMARKET, LONDON, S.W.

(OPPOSITE THE COMEDY THEATRE.)

AWARDED 66 FIRST-CLASS PRIZES, MEDALS AND DIPLOMAS.

Price, 2s. 6d.

1906.

B

OTHER TITLES AVAILABLE THROUGH CONVERPAGE:

0-9728155-0-3 America Illustrated
0-9728155-1-1 The Biography of a Grizzly
0-9728155-5-4 My RV A User's Guide
0-9728155-6-2 The Maritime History of Massachusetts 1783-1860
0-9728155-7-0 An Illustrated Treatise on the Art of Shooting

Visit www.converpage.com and link to www.converpagestore.com for details and pricing. Watch our library grow!

CONVERPAGE SPECIALIZES IN THE REPRODUCTION OF
RARE AND OUT-OF-PRINT BOOKS

ISBN 0-9728155-7-0
An Illustrated Treatise on the Art of Shooting
Digitally Reproduced in 2008 by
CONVERPAGE
23 Acorn Street
Scituate, MA 02066
781-378-1996   www.converpage.com

WALKER & SONS,

MANUFACTURERS. LIMITED.

INSIGNIA OF
FIRST REGIMENT OF RIFLEMEN

ROY S. TINNEY

BUNHILL ROW, LONDON, E.C.,

ESTABLISHED 1848.

GUN FITTING AND INSTRUCTION GIVEN IN THE ART OF SHOOTING BY "EXPERTS."

PANORAMIC VIEW OF CHARLES LANCASTER'S SHOOTING GROUNDS, STONEBRIDGE PARK.

Six Miles from Marble Arch, on the Harrow Road, near Willesden **Junction,** and within ten minutes' walk of Wembley Hill Station, trains from Marylebone Station, Great Central Railway.

Apply to **CHARLES LANCASTER,** 11, Panton Street, Haymarket, London, S.W.

4

FRENCH EDITION, 1898.

———✳———

L'ART DE LA CHASSE
ET
DU TIR.

Traduit par

A. MOURAUX et E. ANDRÉ.

Paris:
SOCIÉTÉ D'EDITIONS SCIENTIFIQUES.
PLACE DE L'ÉCOLE DE MÉDICINE.
4, RUE ANTOINE—DUBOIS 4.

Prix, 7 fr. 50.

SWEDISH EDITION.

———✳———

KONSTEN ATT SKJUTA.

Efter originalits Tridje Upplaga

A F

E. SGK.

Stockholm:

FR. SKOGLUNDS FÖRLAG.

———

Pris, 3 Kronor.

CHARLES LANCASTER'S

NEW PREMISES,

— AT —

11, Panton St., Haymarket, London, S.W.

(OPPOSITE THE COMEDY THEATRE.)

PREFACE TO FIRST EDITION..

At the special request of many gentlemen who have placed themselves in my hands for instruction in the Art of Shooting, I have written this treatise. I have endeavoured to meet the special requirements of those who are anxious to become proficient in the art, and who have hitherto been unable to obtain, in a precise form, the information necessary for studying the first principles of shooting at moving objects.

I have had the honour of coaching many gentlemen, and have carefully studied the points especially requiring attention that have cropped up from time to time while giving instruction. I hope that those who favour me by studying this treatise may quickly gain the knowledge so essential for the making of an average if not brilliant shot.

I have purposely refrained from touching on the several merits of any class of gun—being a gun-maker myself; and, indeed, so many good works on the subject have been written, that it is really unnecessary.

I trust that authors from whose writings I have made extracts will pardon me when they recollect that I have at heart one object, viz., the advancement of a manly sport which gives pleasure, health and occupation to many, and to the patronage of whose followers I am indebted for many pleasant days.

C. L.

1889.

London :
M^cCORQUODALE & CO. LIMITED, PRINTERS,
" THE ARMOURY," SOUTHWARK, S.E.

1903.

❧ OPINIONS OF THE PRESS ❧

FIRST EDITION.

1889.

The book we have now before us, although the work of a gunmaker, is by no means a treatise on the construction of the weapons which it is his business to manufacture, but is a manual of instructions relating to the effective handling of shot guns after they have been made. The author, over and beyond his ordinary business standing, enjoys the reputation of being an excellent "coach," whose endeavour it is, not only " to teach the young idea how to shoot," but likewise to lead men no longer young to abandon old ideas that have proved unconducive to success, and replace them by other methods more likely to attain the desired end. And one purpose of this work is that it may serve as a text-book to pupils, enabling them at their leisure to go again over the ground trodden during the process of personal teaching, and fix in their minds the principles that are sought to be inculcated. But the utility of the book is by no means restricted to those who are self-taught—except in so far as they are observers of men and manners, and imitators of what they conceive to be the best practice—may yet find ample food for reflection in the hints and suggestions that are laid before them.

The book consists of two parts, the first of which may be said to constitute the mainstay of the work ; and in this part will be found, almost exclusively, the numerous illustrations which form its most striking feature. Instead of long verbal descriptions telling the reader what to do, or what not to do—how to carry his gun, say, for use, for comfort, or for safety—a picture is placed before his eyes, showing in action what is inculcated—the grasp of the hand, the posture of the body, and the direction of the barrel ; the figures not being left to the mere imagination of the artist, but the author's ideas being converted into realities by photographic representations of men in the very act of doing what is directed, which photographs have been transferred for printing purposes by the skilful pencil of Mr. J. Temple. There are about fifty of these page-size illustrations, which show how the gun should be carried easily under the arm for a long tramp, or on the shoulder in readiness for immediate use, how to hold it when loading, where the barrel should or should not be directed when walking in line, and what shots ought to be avoided as tending to danger ; how to hit birds that are crossing to right or to left, that are approaching the gun or going straight away, that are skimming low or flying high over the shooter's head, or that have passed beyond him and are going away, with the variations that are required for different angles, as well as for ascending or descending shots, and hints as to when to shoot over birds and when under. The author has preferred to let the illustrations tell their own tale for the most part ; and the defect, if it be one, lies on the side of extreme brevity ; for the pictures in the first portion of the book are so numerous, in comparison with the quantity of text, that the printer has occasionally found himself in straits when endeavouring to place the descriptive matter in front of the corresponding engraving, and consequently, from a typographical point of view, the appearance is not so shapely as it might have been had there been more text to fill out some of the pages.

The second part of the book—which consists partly of original matter and partly of quotations from our own and other pages—touches on subjects less directly connected with the manipulation of the gun in the field. These bring up the volume to about 160 pages of text, exclusive of the illustrations. They include notes on costume, instructions on gun cleaning, measuring for a gun, hammer or hammerless guns, steel and Damascus barrels, chokes and cylinders, times and velocities, sizes of shot, weight of powder charges, and other matters too numerous to particularise. Many of these articles the reader may find more or less interesting, according as his inclination does or does not tend to the study of the theoretical side of shooting questions. But, as we intimated before, the true backbone of the book lies in its first section, which supplies what has long been a *desideratum ;* for, although various authors have briefly touched on the subject, we know of none that will compare with this work for the completeness of its instructive illustrations on the art of handling the gun.—*The Field.*

Our literature possesses no similar work which gives to the embryo shooter or sportsman —and under some circumstances even to those sportsmen who have already handled a gun for some time—such excellent direction how to shoot with sure results for this or that method, or in this or that direction, ground or flying game. Just as instructive as the short and concisely-worded text are the numerous illustrations, which represent and at the same time cause one to understand every possible, imaginable method of the opportunity of shooting, it may be winged or ground game, showing where the sportsman would have to aim in order to make sure of a successful shot in this or that case. . . . . Anyone who interests himself in shooting should not fail to procure the above-mentioned work. . . . . He will, after careful perusal, find it highly instructive and much to be recommended.—*Vienna Sport Zeitung.*

"The Art of Shooting," by Mr. Charles Lancaster, of New Bond Street, is, as might be inferred (coming from the pen of an acknowledged expert), a work which will supply pleasure and profit even to the most skilful gunner ; but to the tyro it will be found to be invaluable. . . . . . Instantaneous photography has lent its marvellous aid to the illustrations with which the book is abundantly supplied.—*Fore's Sporting Notes and Sketches.*

. . . . A well got up volume, written by a practical man in a very practical manner, and freely illustrated.—*The Ironmonger.*

. . . . It is likely to prove of practical service to those who are learning to shoot. . . . . His book has many illustrations, which serve well to elucidate the rules which he lays down.—*Scotsman.*

. . . The book is well illustrated, and highly instructive, and as there are so many who take an interest in shooting, it can hardly fail to command the favour it deserves.—*Sporting Life.*

. . . . The handsomely illustrated volume now before us is exceedingly tasteful in get-up. . . . The drawings are exceedingly instructive. . . . There is much that the most experienced shots in England may read with advantage. . . . It will be a useful book to those who wish to take to shooting. . . . The work under notice deals ably with the subject of carrying one's gun. . . . The sportsman must carry it ready to kill everything but himself or his neighbour or neighbour's dog, and the drawings in the volume before us would be valuable alone, even if unaccompanied by letter-press.—*The County Gentleman.*

. . . . Mr. Charles Lancaster has written an admirable treatise on the "Art of Shooting.' . . . The book is handsomely got up, contains a mass of varied and well-digested information on the subject, and its value is further enhanced by a large number of finely-executed illustrations. . . . Sportsmen . . . cannot do better than read, learn, and inwardly digest Mr. Lancaster's excellent work. Even experts can get many valuable hints from this book.—*Eastern Courier.*

The author modestly refrains from praising or making any allusion to his own weapons. . . . The book is well turned out and printed in excellent type.—*Western Morning News.* . . . This book . . . gives in a number of tersely but capitally drawn illustrations all the hints which experience can suggest. . . . We have the most unmitigated praise to give to the author and to the artist for the manner in which they have brought out this work. The book should be read by every man who shoots . . . it is brimful of practical hints.—*The Shooting Times.*

. . . Mr. Lancaster has, with proper taste, refrained from touching on the merits of any particular class of gun.—*Norfolk Daily Standard.*

. . . We hail with pleasure Mr. Lancaster's book, which is a sort of manual for "teaching the young idea how to shoot," and at the same time showing older hands the necessity of abandoning erroneous notions, and studying the first principles of shooting at moving objects.—*Norwich Argus.*

. . . Altogether the book is well written, and will prove of most valuable assistance to all aspiring sportsmen, and, in fact, will be found of more than ordinary usefulness to those who are already proficient.—*European Mail.*

. . . Mr. Lancaster, whose name is well known in connection with shooting, has issued a short treatise on this branch of sport which is likely to prove acceptable to many. . . . Mr. Lancaster's book is a useful compendium of knowledge for the beginner, from which even the practised sportsman may gather some invaluable hints.—*Morning Post.*

. . . A remarkably useful book for all wishing to learn how to use a gun properly. . . . After a careful read through the book, I must say that, although nothing of a sportsman myself, I really believe that, following the advice given, and with a little practice, I could soon become a very fair shot. The whole matter is dealt with most thoroughly.—*Colonies and India.*

. . . A useful work to all those who wish to shoot well and in sportsmanlike fashion. . . . The writer has spared no pains in dealing with his subject.—*Home and Colonial Mail.*

. . . Much time and vexation may be saved by careful attention to the advice of a judicious "coach." Mr. Lancaster goes patiently over the minutest points. . . . Hence the treatise will be found instructive and useful.—*Daily Chronicle.*

. . . In his excellently written and fully illustrated pages Mr. Lancaster deals scientifically and practically with the whole question of guns and shooting, quoting from his wide experience, and also making extracts from other authoritative writers on the subject. The result is a work which might well become a recognised text-book on the art of shooting. . . The book is full of technical hints, and its numerous illustrations are an admirable aid to a complete apprehension of the text.—*Court Journal.*

. . . Mr. Charles Lancaster, the well-known gunmaker, has prepared a very useful little treatise on shooting, admirably adapted not only for those who are commencing to handle a gun, but also those who have failed, for want of proper instructions, to advance beyond a condition of mediocrity. The remarks are well explained by effective engravings.—*Colburn's United Service Magazine.*

Since "The Deadshot" was written many years ago, we have had no work on the practical use of the fowling-piece until the present treatise of Mr. Chas. Lancaster. . . . Mr. Lancaster is evidently a clever and ardent sportsman ; he has had to learn, has learnt, and now teaches well, and the lessons given must be of immense value to the ordinary as well as to the inexperienced sportsman. We have no hesitation in saying that the author's instructions on the art of shooting are the most valuable that have ever been placed before the public, and the illustrations which accompany them are pre-eminently illustrative of the text, which is saying a great deal. Author and artist have worked together to produce an excellent and valuable result. . . . Altogether, "The Art of Shooting" is a valuable and pleasant addition to the sporting library. It is a book every sportsman has been in want of, and which every sportsman ought to possess.—*The Bazaar, Exchange and Mart.*

There is a great deal of practical information in the illustrated treatise written and published by Mr. Charles Lancaster upon "The Art of Shooting," and the lucid and comprehensive text is supplemented by a number of clever sketches, reproduced from instantaneous photographs. . . . The book is a well written and reliable handy guide, and is worthy of careful study.—*Daily Telegraph.*

The art of shooting, or rather that part of it which is concerned with moving objects, is dealt with fairly exhaustively in Mr. Lancaster's book. . . . The illustrations, too, are particularly good. . . . Some very useful practical information on guns and other shooting gear is given. . . . The book ought to be read by every sportsman, from the merest tyro to the veteran "shot." The one will gain much instruction, and the other not a little amusement and edification.—*The British Trade Journal.*

. . . Mr. Lancaster, who is reputed a good "coach" at shooting, as well as a maker of first-class guns, has acceded to a frequent request that he should write a book on shooting. The result is admirable. No one can help being favourably impressed, to begin with, by the design of the work. . . . He is always entertaining as well as instructive. His book is singularly agreeable.—*Rod and Gun.*

Mr. Charles Lancaster is well known as an accomplished "coach" for men who wish to acquire the art of shooting game, and he is, moreover, a practical gun-maker ; he therefore may claim to write as an expert. . . . The illustrations, admirably drawn by Mr. J. Temple, from instantaneous photographs, are very good indeed.—*Manchester Guardian.*

. . . Mr. Lancaster here supplies us with a *desideratum* which, as we have said, will be welcomed by all who desire to become proficient in the art of handling the gun.—*Lowestoft Standard.*

. . . . The fifty illustrations by Mr. James Temple . . . show how the gun should be held when in and out of use. These pictures are a considerable help to students puzzling their brain over lengthy descriptions of what to do and what not to do.—*Norfolk Weekly Standard.*

. . . We say, read what Mr. Charles Lancaster has to tell in respect to the study and practice of his lifetime. . . . We have frequently heard the complaint of a dearth in artistic records of the manner in which shooting is carried on at the present time. This want Mr. Lancaster supplies, with no niggard hand ; and we peruse his chapters and gaze, fondly at his sketches with long and lingering eye, wishing, like Oliver Twist, for more. The author, like a good "coach," commences *ab initio*, and, after a few apposite and general remarks, gives us, in good plain English, a number of sound hints and maxims as to the science he himself has mastered. . . . We should be manifestly ungrateful to the artist, Mr. Temple, were we not to acknowledge how loyally he has illustrated the meaning and the text of the author in the various sketches he has given. To say they are true to nature is to speak of these little pictures as works of art worthy of Leech, Irving, Tenniel or "Sir Edwin ; " and it is no flattery to give them this rank.—*The Broad Arrow.*

"The Art of Shooting" is a useful and well illustrated little treatise.—*Yorkshire Post.*

. . . The book is full of original and collected matter, and the reader will pick up many hints as to the shooting of birds on the wing and of hares and rabbits. . . . A generally useful book.—*The Army and Navy Gazette.*

The "Art of Shooting" should be perused by all sportsmen desirous to become good shots.—*The Critic.*

There is a great deal of good advice in Mr. C. Lancaster's treatise. . . . With a delicacy rare in such books, he abstains from recommending any particular kind of gun.—*The Graphic.*

Mr. C. Lancaster's treatise on "The Art of Shooting," has been published for the benefit of his pupils, and may possibly be useful to them as others than his lectures.—*The World.*

. . . This is a good book for beginners, no doubt, and is certainly well and profusely illustrated.—*The Weekly Bulletin.*

. . . This is a practical manual by an expert in the art which it is intended to teach. The instructions are conveyed in a brief and pithy form. . . . The best authorities are cited by Mr. Lancaster in support of his views, and indeed he speaks himself from an exceptionally varied experience, not only as a sportsman, but as a teacher in the use of firearms. —*Home News.*

. . . They (experts) would be the first, therefore, to praise Mr. Lancaster for the pains he has taken to explain simple principles and to illustrate details. . . . Mr. Lancaster does valuable service in devoting so much attention to them. . . . A careful study of Mr. Lancaster's book, and the aid of many illustrations very skilfully drawn by Mr. James Temple, will give even proficient sportsmen a clearer insight into theoretical principles than could be gained by any ordinary means. . . . The author's success as a practical gun-maker in overcoming difficulties of this kind entitles him to speak with authority, and it must be said that he is not chary in giving the fruits of his wide experience to those who care to cull valuable hints from the treatise written and published by him. . . . Words of warning are given to sportsmen whose carelessness in carrying dangerous weapons and reck-lessness in shooting without regard for others deserve even severer censure than Mr. Lancaster administers.—*Illustrated London News.*

. . . It is a nicely got-up and well-printed book ; . . . it is, therefore with pleasure, that we welcome the words of wisdom and advice from such a practical man, keen sportsman, and tutor of many good shots, as Mr. Lancaster. . . . In conclusion, we can only urge those of our readers who are and are not, and those who would be sportsmen, to obtain a copy of this valuable work.—*Sale and Exchange.*

To many sportsmen the idea of learning to shoot from a book may seem analogous to acquiring the noble art of self-defence by sparring at one's reflection in a mirror ; but it must be conceded that Mr. Charles Lancaster's Book of Instructions affords many useful hints, not only to the novice, but to older hands. . . . Mr. Lancaster's directions have the merit, at any rate, of simplicity ; and instead of elaborate and complicated diagrams, he gives us full-page illustrations of the sportsman firing at feather and fur in almost every possible flight and run. . . . A very interesting chapter is devoted to " times and velocities," and the author shows how the question of " allowance " is effected by the difference of nervous organisation in sportsmen.—*The Leeds Mercury.*

. . . The name of Charles Lancaster is familiar to most shooting men, and a work on shooting written by one of the leading West End gunmakers—himself a capital shot—does not need much praise to recommend it. . . . The clear way in which the author directs his pupil how, when, and where to shoot at birds flying at all kinds of angles, cannot fail to assist him greatly.—*Teignmouth Post.*

Mr. Lancaster's book is practical. It is exactly what it professes to be—a book for those who wish to learn to shoot, and who have not the time necessary for going through a long course of education in the fields and woods. Even to such as have, however, it will be found extremely useful ; for it is not true of shooting that practice makes perfect, and many a man may go on shooting every day of his life and never shoot well to the end of it for the want of some judicious instruction from a master of the craft. Mr. Lancaster passes in review every kind of shot that can present itself. . . . and gives appropriate rules for each, which are further impressed on us by means of very useful illustrations.—*St. James's Gazette.*

. . . Written by such an authority, this book cannot fail to be of value. . . . To the large majority, however, the hints given will prove most useful. . . . Every kind of shot is described. . . . There is much in it that is practical.—*Admiralty and Horse Guards' Gazette.*

. . . Contains a mass of information about the use of the gun, and is copiously illustrated. . . . The work may be safely recommended to all and sundry anxious to become " cracks," for the manner of paragraphing special bits of advice is admirable, and enables anybody to see at a glance what is meant. A word must be said for the printing of this useful volume, which is really most excellent.—*The Sportsman.*

. . . One purpose of this work is that it may serve as a text-book. . . . Supplies what has long been a *desideratum.* . . . We know of none that will compare with the work for the completeness of its illustrations on the art of handling the gun.—*Brighton Gazette.*

. . . This work will be found an invaluable aid to proficiency in the art of shooting. The author is not only a practical gunmaker . . . but is also a thoroughly practical sportsman, so that his qualifications for a work of this description leave nothing to be desired. . . . Indeed, it should be found on the bookshelf of all who " handle " a gun.—*American Traveller.*

. . . This book is capitally got up, copiously illustrated, and is a compendium of information on the subject on which it treats.—*Calcutta Asian.*

Charles Lancaster, one of the first authorities on guns, has just written an admirable treatise which cannot fail to be of value . . . the hints given will prove most useful . . . the book is sure to command, as it deserves a wide circulation.—*Irish Times.*

. . . There is no one living who can so well impart information on the art of wing shooting as Mr. Lancaster . . . as this volume is not written to puff the Lancaster gun, it is sure to be well received in America. . . . I most cheerfully recommend this volume . . . no intelligent sportsman will regret the time or money it has cost him.—" GAUCHO." —*American Breeder and Sportsman.,*

. . . A very useful book . . . which will be serviceable to many besides the mere tyro. . . . Mr. Lancaster's diagrams show us our theory in practice, and help to fix in the memory maxims which are apt to escape us at the critical moment when conveyed only in words.—*Blackwood's Magazine.*

Contents.

PART I.

CONTENTS—*continued.*

Illustrations.

The original Illustrations were drawn by JAS. and GEO. TEMPLE, from instantaneous and other Photographs, taken at Charles Lancaster's Private Shooting Grounds, by Messrs. R. & H. STILES, of Campden Hill Road, Kensington, and others.

THE ART OF SHOOTING.

PART I.

GENERAL INFORMATION.

AMONG the requisites for successful shooting is, first of all, judgment of pace—or, in other words, the rate at which the object to be shot is travelling; then getting the proper allowance, so as to ensure the charge of shot from the gun being put exactly where this moving object is likely to be on impact—in the same way as a school-boy learns instinctively by practice, when playing such a game as rounders, where to throw the ball so as to hit or " scorch " the individual running.

Secondly, angles have to be considered; and I have in the accompanying sketches endeavoured to put them in as simple a form as possible, so that those wishing to see them clearly may do so. These angles

have been worked at and proved correct after much
study and hard work, and will, I hope, save the
novice much trouble : they may never have had
a thought bestowed on them before, and yet they
are most essential for the purpose of becoming a
good shot.

Thirdly, the sense of touch plays a most important
part in shooting. In the use of a gun, the instant
the sight and aim have done their work, the finger
must pull the trigger to discharge the gun ; if too
hard in the pull-off, time is lost and the judgment
beaten ; if too light, the gun may be discharged too
soon, and possibly not " within a mile " of the place
where the sight and aim had intended it should be
placed at the impact of the charge and shot on the
object to be struck.

Lastly, a good fit in a gun is as necessary for a
successful shot as a well-fitting shoe is for a pedes-
trian. Some men are smaller than others, and a man
must have his gun to fit him the same as his clothes ;
consequently the gun that fits one may not fit
another. Men's likes and dislikes, too, are as
different as their faces, and what suits one will not
suit another. To test if a gun is really a fit, pin a piece
of white paper on a wall or a tree, then put the gun

Missing by " Skying " with a Stock too Long and Straight.

up at it quickly, with both eyes open, and after several such trials one can tell how the gun suits. If it mounts too high, the stock is too straight (*see Ill. No. 1, page 13*)—if low, the stock is too bent if to the left, stock should be cast-off to the right— if to the right, it should be cast-on to the left; if the stock catches in bringing it up on the object, it is too long and wants shortening (*see Ill. No. 1, page 13*). To ascertain the latter, by leaning forward from the hips a gun that is too long can be mounted to its proper place, and by gradually returning to the upright position, until the gun catches, the excess of length may be demonstrated. A tall man will require more bend and length than a shorter one; and a stout man will require more cast-off than a thin one. In selecting a gun the buyer must at all times bear in mind that there is a handicap in weight and bore of guns, as in all sports where fatigue and accuracy come in; therefore one man can use a gun at 7 or $7\frac{1}{2}$ lbs., whereas another can only carry, say, 6 lbs. But a 12-bore gun of 6 lbs., or under, must, as a scientific necessity, recoil and jump more than the heavier ones; it is better therefore to use a smaller load, or a gun of smaller bore, than to shoot with a gun that is very likely to tell its tale against you in excessive recoil, because no one can shoot even moderately well if he is getting punished.

Some of the matters here briefly touched upon will be dealt with more fully in subsequent pages.

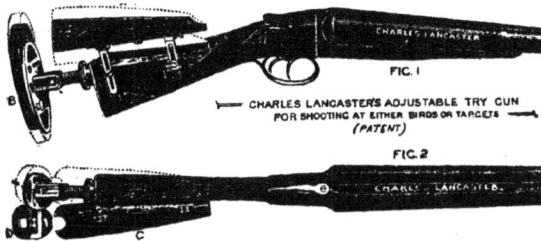

CHARLES LANCASTER'S ADJUSTABLE "TRY GUNS," either with the Ordinary 2 Triggers, or with Patent Single Trigger.

NOTE.—The author has invented an adjustable try-gun (patent), which is constructed with the stock perfectly rigid in the hand, being made to move in right lines (and *not* bodily, by the means of a knuckle-joint in the hand of stock, which necessarily describes the section of a circle), therefore the author's does not give an excess of bend or cast-off, yet it can be adjusted for cast-off, bend, and length, also for set of toe or heel of stock, so as to be correctly adjusted to what is required for any individual sportsman, to enable him to make accurate practice when firing at either targets or game ; or the author's original adjustable gun (with specially constructed fittings) can be handled to demonstrate that the measurements taken by him are correct as to bend, length, and cast-off, thereby showing that the gun to be supplied will be suited to the purchaser.

SIGHT AND ITS PECULIARITIES.

To make an average shot, it is first absolutely necessary to be in a condition to see clearly any object up to, say, 50 yards.

Those who cannot see to shoot without spectacles should use those having the glasses or pebbles made circular, with a diameter of not less than $1\frac{1}{2}$ inches, and well set out from the face at the lower part, so that when the head is in the correct position, with the gun at the shoulder, the surfaces of the glasses are at right angles to the barrels. Then it must be ascertained which eye is the master, or, in other words, whether it is the right or left eye that finds the object most quickly.

To ascertain this, take an ordinary finger ring, and hold it out at some distance from the face, so that a small object (*see Ills.* Nos. 2 and 3, pages 18 and 19) can be seen through it about five or six yards distant, keeping both eyes open. Keep the hand and ring perfectly steady, then close the left eye, and if the right eye sees the object as exactly central through the ring, that is the master eye (see fig. 1). Then open the left eye and close the right; the line of sight through the ring, as shown in the red line (fig. 1), will incline to the right towards A, that was seen to be central when using the right eye with the left closed (*see Ill. No. 2, fig. 1*).

Then reverse the operation (fig. 2) but after focussing the object (see fig. 2) through the ring, keeping the hand and ring perfectly steady, close the right eye, and if the left eye sees the object as exactly central through the ring, then the left is the master eye (see fig. 2). Then open the right eye, and close the left; this should cause the line of sight through the ring, as shown in the red line (fig. 2), to be carried some distance to the left hand (to letter A, fig. 2), that was seen to be centrally aligned when using the left eye with the right closed (*see Ill. No. 2, fig. 2*).

c

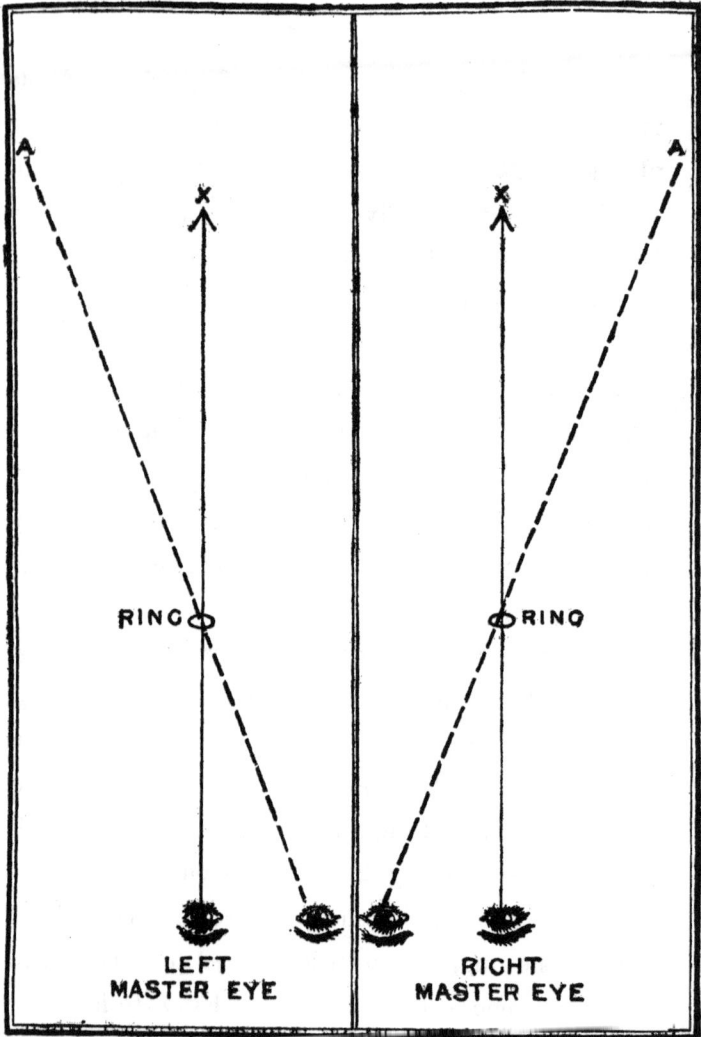

LEFT
MASTER EYE

RIGHT
MASTER EYE

RING

RING

X

X

A

A

FIG 2.

FIG I.

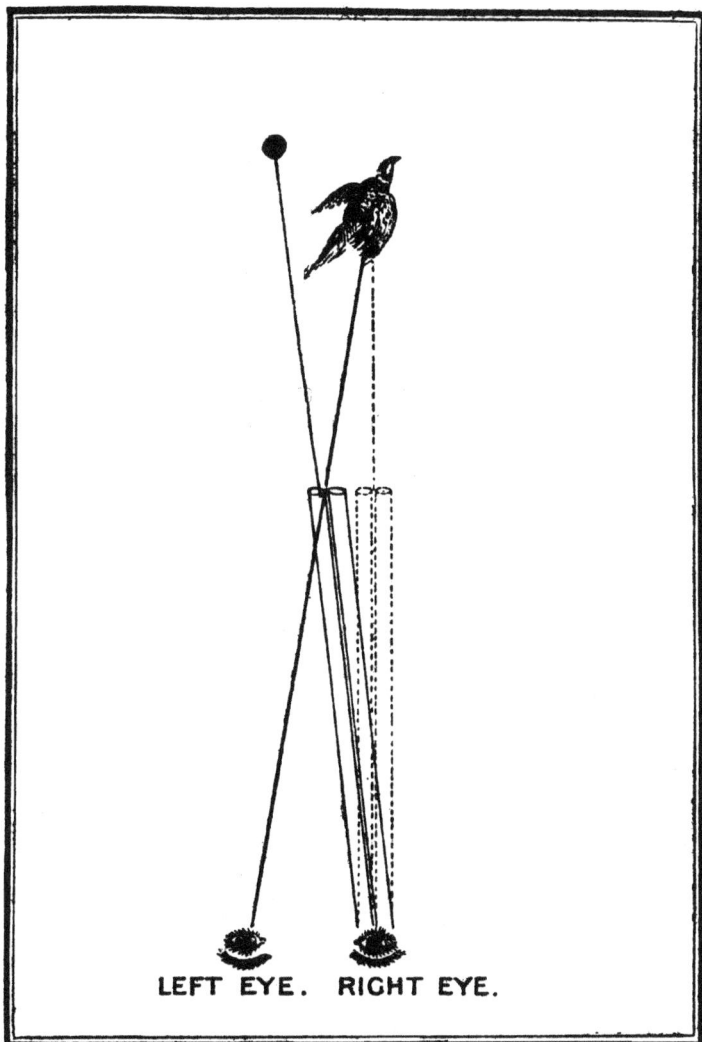

LEFT EYE.   RIGHT EYE.

Effect of "Aiming" with both eyes open, the left being
the Master eye.

No man with a more powerful left eye than the right can be expected to take a perfect alignment with the right eye, or to shoot with a gun, unless the centre of the rib of the barrels comes absolutely opposite to it.* If he has a right-eyed gun, the left being the master eye, it would cause him to shoot from 1 to 12 feet to the left of the object, according to the distance he gets away (*see* red line, *Ill.* No. 3, page 19). To correct this error, he must close the left eye, causing the gun to be brought from point O back to cover properly the bird, so that in shooting at an object crossing from R to L he would be ahead of it, and with a better chance of hitting it, but if crossing from L to R he would be a great deal behind it, and consequently miss it. This may be owing to too little cast-off even to a right-eyed man.† The subject of cast-off, however, can hardly be treated of fully at this point, and will be referred to again hereafter.

---

* I find, since the publication of the First and Second Editions, that this question has sorely puzzled many sportsmen, therefore I give the following suggestions, hoping that they may assist those having a more powerful left eye : 1st. Close the left eye *before* the gun is put to the shoulder, so as to allow of the right eye " fixing " or thoroughly observing the object. 2nd. Use a gun with sufficient cast-off for the *left* eye to align from the *right* shoulder. 3rd. Have spectacles made so as to increase the power of the right eye, so that it may equal or be better than the left. (N.B.—This should not be attempted without consulting an Oculist). 4th. Shoot from the left shoulder and left eye, the gun being specially adjusted for this purpose.

† In some instances it has been found advantageous to cast-off a gun sufficiently so as to be correctly aligned for both eyes, and which is called a " central vision " gun. But this can only be properly adjusted by the actual test of aiming and shooting at a target with both eyes open (not taking a snap shot) to ascertain if the shot strikes the object in view.

CARRYING AND LOADING A GUN.

I consider it half the battle, where a gun has to be carried all day, over good or bad ground, to understand the easiest method of doing so without undue fatigue, and therefore I submit the illustrations (Nos. 4 and 5) as being likely to convey the idea without a long wordy description; but I prefer the manner so well shown in illustration (No. 5, page 23) —where the gun is being carried on the right shoulder and hand—because it admits of the gun being brought to cover an object immediately without changing the hold or grasp of the stock.

But please note that often barrels are dented and damaged when two sportsmen are side by side (*see Ill.* No. 6, page 24) ; then it is better to let the gun rest on the arm, either with or without the gun being open, the latter a safe and convenient way.

Carrying for a Long Tramp.

Carrying, yet Ready.

Often Barrels are dented and damaged when two Sportsmen are side by side; then it is better to let the Gun rest on the arm, either with or without the Gun being open, the latter a safe and convenient way.

Convenient Holding for Loading.

Closing the Gun by the toe of the stock, a
safe way for "Loaders" and "Guns."

Closing the wrong way, the Cartridges
falling out.

No. 8]

[26

A YOUNG BEGINNER.

(Aged 4½, 1894.)

LEARNING HIS TRADE AT THE BENCH 1905.

The position for loading a gun, or placing it to
half-cock or " safe," should be carefully studied—not
only with a view to ease in loading, but more
especially that, when in the act of opening the gun
to reload (*see Ill.* No. 7, page 25) after having only
fired one barrel, or in closing the gun when reloaded,*
the barrels may never by the slightest chance be
allowed to cover or point near dog or man.   This I
wish especially to impress upon everyone's mind,
whether beg·nner or not, because I have noticed it
frequently occur.   Should the gun go off by accident,
when the gun is pointed in a clear direction, no harm
can be done; whereas, if carelessly pointed, a sad
loss of limb or life may take place.

* *See Ill.* No. 8, Page 26.

"TEACHING THE YOUNG IDEA TO SHOOT."

From " Country Life Illustrated" October 20th, 1900.

Dear Mr Editor

Father has given me a beautiful gun, and is teaching me how to shoot. He says it is so cruel to only wound poor little bunnies or birds so I must try to shoot straight. I send you a photograph, and hope you will think I am holding my gun properly I am eight years old.

Your little friend
"A chip of the old block"
S. A. T.

To the Editor of
Country Life
Tavistock Street
W. C.

BOYS' GUNS A SPECIALITY.

HANDLING AND POSITION.

At all times it is best, and most essential, to get a firm hold of the gun with both hands; but care must be taken to notice that, as the left hand has generally to come over to the right side for a correct alignment, you should not hold the barrels too forward, or the left hand will not come over, and will tend to check the gun from taking a true and square shot, especially so on the right. At all times be careful that you have both feet well placed, the left foot slightly in advance of the right, but in an easy position; the body bending forward so that the chin plumbs the left foot—the knees never bent (*see Ills.* Nos. 9, 10 and 11), and the weight of the body on the left foot, the heel of the right slightly raised.

The First Position.

No. 9]

No. 10]   The Second Position.   [82

No. 11]   Faced to the Right.   [33

D

Should, by any chance, a bird go to right or left, be careful to make a complete change of front, *i.e.*, either to left or right half-turn; and always be careful to use the right foot as the pivot, moving only the left from the ground—turning on the right by moving the body to the direction of the flight of the bird (*see Ill.* No. 11, page 33). This allows the body to be square to it, and prevents an unpleasant recoil on the arm, or perhaps a kick on the face, which may be felt the next few shots and cause the shooter to flinch.

Never draw back the right foot; because by doing so the tendency is to draw the gun down too low, thereby causing the shot to go under or behind. In taking up a position at the covert side always find a firm footing—for choice, the left foot should be lower than the right, as it will naturally tend to throw the body forward. The body being forward (*see Ill.* No. 10, page 32) gives greater resistance for the recoil of the first barrel, and allows the gun to mount cleaner without fear of catching, and the body will then be in the upright position for the second; but if the first barrel is fired with the body erect, the recoil will tend to place the body out of balance, and this takes time to correct. The loss of a second means that the bird may have travelled 15 or 20 yards, thereby preventing the chance of a second shot at a reasonable distance.

Nº 2.

Nº 3

Nº 1.

Nº 4.

Nº 5

Gun Cabinets.

I.—Walk with Barrels well up, and laying towards the left.

II.—Walking ceased Barrels thrown over to the right side ready to be put to the shoulder.

III.—Weight of body thrown on left foot, and gun brought smartly to the shoulder.

No. 13]

[37

ELEMENTARY PRACTICE.

"Practice makes perfect," is a true and old adage; and in shooting, as in all other sports where ease of movement combined with well-hardened sinews and muscles are requisite, those who practice most will become proficient first. I advise the handling of a gun once or twice a week all the year round, if even for only ten minutes at a time; but oftener than this is necessary for a beginner.

With a view of assisting the beginner (and others) to overcome the flurry when game rises, and the consequent careless bringing of the gun to the shoulder, whereby the degree of exactness with which it should be done is spoilt, I insert illustrations (No. 13), arranged numerically, in which these position exercises should be made, and so admit of a good view to be taken of the object to be shot; and hope they will be as useful in assisting my readers to overcome the faults mentioned as they have been to those of my patrons whom I have personally instructed at my private shooting grounds, see page 44, so much so, that whereas previously birds had been missed with both barrels, subsequently a right and left had been easily taken with the coolness exhibited by a first-class shot.

When you have a gun, don't forget where it is, but keep it in some handy, get-at-able place. Many who really feel inclined to practice, often do not do so, because "it's too much bother to get it from the gun-case," etc., etc.—whereas, if it is always kept within reach, there is no excuse to be made, and the work is done (*see Ill.* No. 12, on page 36, and inside cover).

To the beginner, I say, be most careful how you commence, so as not to get into a bad position (*see Ill.* No. 14, page 40), because that makes the work much more difficult, and very tiring. Take the gun in both hands, the right well held round the hand of the stock, and the left well forward—just to the tip of the fore-end if possible—so that, when the gun is mounted to the shoulder, the left arm is well stretched out (*see Ill.* No. 10, page 32). Be careful to stand well on the feet. Stand in the first position —that is, with the heels touching, and the toes about 6–10 inches apart ; then move the left foot half-a-step forward, and bend the body forward from the hips, so that the chin will plumb the left toe. This will allow the body to be at a convenient angle for the gun to be brought quickly to the shoulder (*see Ill.* No. 10, page 32), at the same time giving resistance for the recoil of the gun, allowing the balance to be kept, and enabling a second barrel to be fired quickly and conveniently when shooting. Then handle and mount the gun to the shoulder, keeping both eyes open and facing some object in the room (such as a picture nail)—do this quickly some few times, taking care to have the finger on the right-hand trigger, ready to pull as soon as the gun is at the shoulder (*see Ill.* No. 11, page 33).

Bad Positions—to be avoided.

Preparing for the First Shot at a Mark.

To get a fair pull of the trigger, the finger should be bent, with the first joint resting lightly on the trigger, so as to prevent a snatch pull; and see that the other part of the finger is not touching the stock, or it will cause the pull to be too heavy, and draw the gun out of alignment.

Press the gun to the shoulder with considerable force as it is mounted; this should be done in one movement. After working this covering of the object, swing the gun to another selected mark at about 12 to 15 feet to the left of the first; continue to do this, reversing the movement left to right. Repeat this mode of practice on and off for some days, and then you will be in a position to fire a few shots at a mark in the open, either on a wall or shot-proof screen made for the purpose (*see Ill.* No. 15, page 41).

In shooting at such a mark, walk three or four steps towards it before firing; and never fire if you feel you are not covering the object you desire to hit. This will enable you to observe what you are doing each time, and allow of corrections being made.

When the fixed mark can be hit pretty frequently, the beginner can proceed to practising at moving objects.

INANIMATE MOVING OBJECTS.

There are many excellent Traps on the market at the present time, also the celebrated and improved " Expert " Traps and " Clay " (*i.e.* composition) Pigeons, which afford the best means of getting practice shooting at inanimate moving objects (*see Ill.* No. 16, page 46).

The beginner can place the trap so that the " Clay " Pigeons will be thrown forward, to the right or left, high or low, or can have the trap worked by an attendant from behind a wall or shot-proof fence—somewhat after the flight of driven birds, or even for high in-coming shots—from a suitable tower or building.

Pitch composition balls, as used by " Buffalo Bill " at the American Exhibition—with an attendant standing ready to throw them from the side of the beginner in different directions—also afford good practice ; moreover these balls cannot leave any objectionable pieces, likely to damage the feet of cattle, dogs, etc., as is the case with glass balls. The Author supplies special gun-metal moulds for casting these balls, so that a gentleman having a mould can make the balls at home, thereby saving loss by breakage whilst in transit.

HIGH TOWER —Receiving Instruction.
Giving a lesson at Charles Lancaster's Shooting Grounds.

SHOOTING SCHOOLS.

Reprinted from *The County Gentleman*, May 30th, 1903.

Boy, 13 Years of Age, having Practice and Instruction during the Easter Vacation at Charles Lancaster's Private Shooting Grounds, Stonebridge, near Willesden Junction, N.W.

The accompanying illustration, obtained from Mr. Lancaster, shows a youth of 13½ years of age engaged in practice at "clay" birds in these grounds. The gun he is using in the photograph is a double 20-bore hammerless ejector, weighing 5 lbs., and loaded with 28 grs. of Schultze, and ¾ oz. of medium game shot.

[45

No. 16]   Annie Oakley Practising at Clay Pigeons.   [46

BIRDS ON THE WING.

After the beginner finds that he can break " Clay " Pigeons, Pitch Balls, or other inanimate objects, he may proceed to obtain further practice by shooting at small birds, such as starlings, sparrows, etc., either released from a trap or thrown up by an attendant (*see Ill.* No. 18, page 49).

One need not become what is generally known as a " trap-shot " from this method; but by knowing from where a bird will be sprung, a beginner is enabled to become cool and collected, and to take time to see the " flying bird " well on the wing before he need shoot—especially if he will walk six to ten paces before having the " bird " released, watch its flight until it has got a fair distance, and then shoot. Then, when a fair score can be made, two " birds " may be released from separate traps, one just before the other, so as to enable the beginner to get a " right " and " left," and to keep the firing of the second barrel within a fair time of the first. Afterwards both " birds " may be released simultaneously.

Trap Shooting—" Are you Ready?"

E

Original Text for Shooting Birds and "Clays" at Charles Lancaster's Shooting Grounds.

CHARLES LANCASTER'S PRIVATE SHOOTING GROUNDS

STONE BRIDGE, WILLESDEN, N.W.

LANCASTER

RABBIT SHOOTING

MOVING PRACTICE FOR ROCKETERS
SINGLE OR DOUBLE RISE CLAY PIGEON'S
AT CLAY OR LIVE BIRDS PROJECTED
FROM HIGH TOWER

PIGEON

MOVING TARGET

GUN FITTING WITH ADJUSTABLE TRY GUN

LESSONS AND PRACTICE IN ALL KINDS OF SHOOTING GIVEN AT ABOVE SHOOTING GROUNDS.

ALL COMMUNICATIONS FOR APPOINTMENTS, &c., TO BE ADDRESSED TO

11, PANTON STREET, HAYMARKET, LONDON, S.W.

TELEPHONE: 8691 GERRARD.

No. 19]
Keeping the Gun to the Shoulder for a "Right" and "Left."
[51

Many persons fail in shooting from inability to judge distance. I therefore recommend that, before two "birds" are released, good-sized bunches of newspaper should be left on the ground, say at 30 and 40 yards from where the shooter is standing. With practice this will teach what law a bird should have, and when not to shoot, owing to the bird having flown out of range.

Do not take the gun down from the shoulder between the two shots (*see Ill.* No. 19, page 51), because it loses much time, and the bird may have flown out of range ; or, in driving, a second shot may be lost forward, the most deadly and correct way to take driven birds.

SHOOTING WINGED GAME.

A great difficulty here presents itself to the Author, because this Treatise is not written with a view of telling the sportsman how shootings should be managed, game reared and found, or ground worked to obtain the best results. Many good works have been written on these subjects, and I refer my readers to the works enumerated on page 216. I will, however, just mention a few of the most important facts to be remembered.

Be careful to carry your gun in such a way that it never covers your left-hand " gun " (*see Ills*. Nos. 22 and 23), because it is not pleasant to find the line being broken in walking, owing to the left " guns " hanging back to escape looking down the muzzles of your barrels.

Be careful never to shoot across your next gun nor take his bird (*see Ill*. No. 25, page 59).

In covert, just as much care should be taken, as the careless handling of a gun by one may spoil the enjoyment of a whole party. Etiquette of the field often prevents a word of caution being given to a careless man, although a retiring or shrinking away from the line of his gun may have the desired effect (*see Ills*. Nos. 20 and 23, pages 54 to 57).

Always allow pheasants to rise sufficiently to prevent a dangerously low shot being taken. (See *Ill*. No. 24, page 58.)

Standing in Covert.—Dangerous to others.

Walking in Line to a " Point " (Position I.)
Gun well forward—correctly, and safe to others.

Walking in Line (Position II.)—Correctly, and safe to others; barrels well up.

Walking in Line—Dangerous to others.

No. 24]   [58

A Dangerously low Shot in Covert.

Never Shoot across, nor take another's Bird.

A nice Angle to take at.

A Dangerous Shot.

Once one of a party managed to give me a good " dusting " under the following circumstances :— A rabbit was seen in the covert we were facing, when suddenly it bolted out into the ride and came towards me in a direct line. I saw the next " gun " about to shoot. I shouted, " Don't shoot ! " but too late ; he had fired ; the shot glanced from the stony ride and " dusted " me all down one side (*see Ill.* No. 27, page 61).

This shot was made by a man who should have known better ; and it so impressed itself on my mind that I cannot help mentioning it here, as a caution to others who might be tempted to fire such a shot. Many persons may probably have had a similar unpleasant experience.

THE PERPENDICULAR SHOT.

To shoot birds well overhead, or perfectly perpendicular, is one of the most telling and prettiest
shots to be made (*see Ill.* No. 28, page 64), but one
requiring great coolness and practice. * When learnt,
however, such a shot is not difficult, as by waiting it
gives plenty of time to get ready—the bird having
been seen, at some distance away, as it approaches.

When shot in this way the birds are more often
well killed, as they present the most vulnerable
parts to the shooter. If birds are flying at a great
pace, and high, a good allowance in front must be
made, or the bird will be missed. See Chapter on
Flight of Birds, page 188.

NOTE.—See pages 201 and 202, for Article from *The Field*, on
" Penetration of Shot at ' Tall ' Pheasants."

* Excellent means for this practice can now be had at Charles
Lancaster's Shooting Grounds, where there is a specially constructed
high tower, 30 ft. above the surrounding trees, from which " Clay " Birds
can be projected at great speed, and in any direction. (See page 67,
Ill. No. 31).

Shooting well back overhead.

Watching them coming high—back from roots into covert

How to get them well overhead.

HIGH TOWER—30 feet above surrounding Trees, at Charles Lancaster's
Shooting Grounds.

Standing perfectly steady (*see Ill.* No. 29, page 65), and watching the bird approach until it is nearly overhead, the body must then be thrown back so that the whole of its weight is on the right leg, the left toes just touching the ground, so as to steady the shooter (*see Ill.* No. 30, page 66), the left hand being brought down the barrel nearer to the right, so as to allow of the gun being pushed well in line of the right shoulder and right eye; or else the gun will be drawn to the left, and so be out of proper alignment, consequently causing the shot to go all to the left.

Few sportsmen are seen to do this class of shooting really well. Many fail because they do not practice the movement sufficiently before they go out, and consequently do not get far enough back —being too stiff; also, because they do not get far enough ahead of the bird at the instant of pulling, but check the gun perceptibly.

Excellent practice may be had by placing an "Expert" trap (*see Ill.* 31, page 67), on a hay-rick or out-building about 20 to 50 feet high, and then sending the "clay" pigeons well over the shooter's head, the shooter facing the trap and tower.

THE APPROACHING SHOT.

This is really not a difficult shot to learn, and may be divided into three kinds—the approaching high shot, *i.e.*, above the level of the sportsman's head, the approaching low shot, *i.e.*, below the level of his head, and the direct, *i.e.*, straight on.

The high shot must be made by shooting well in front of the bird's head, if fairly close ; but if further away—say 35 to 40 yards—less allowance must be given, because the flight of the charge of shot is more streaming and parallel than if directly overhead and closer. Many miss these shots by shooting too much at the bird, and not swinging the gun ahead at the moment of pulling (*see Ill.* No. 32, page 70).

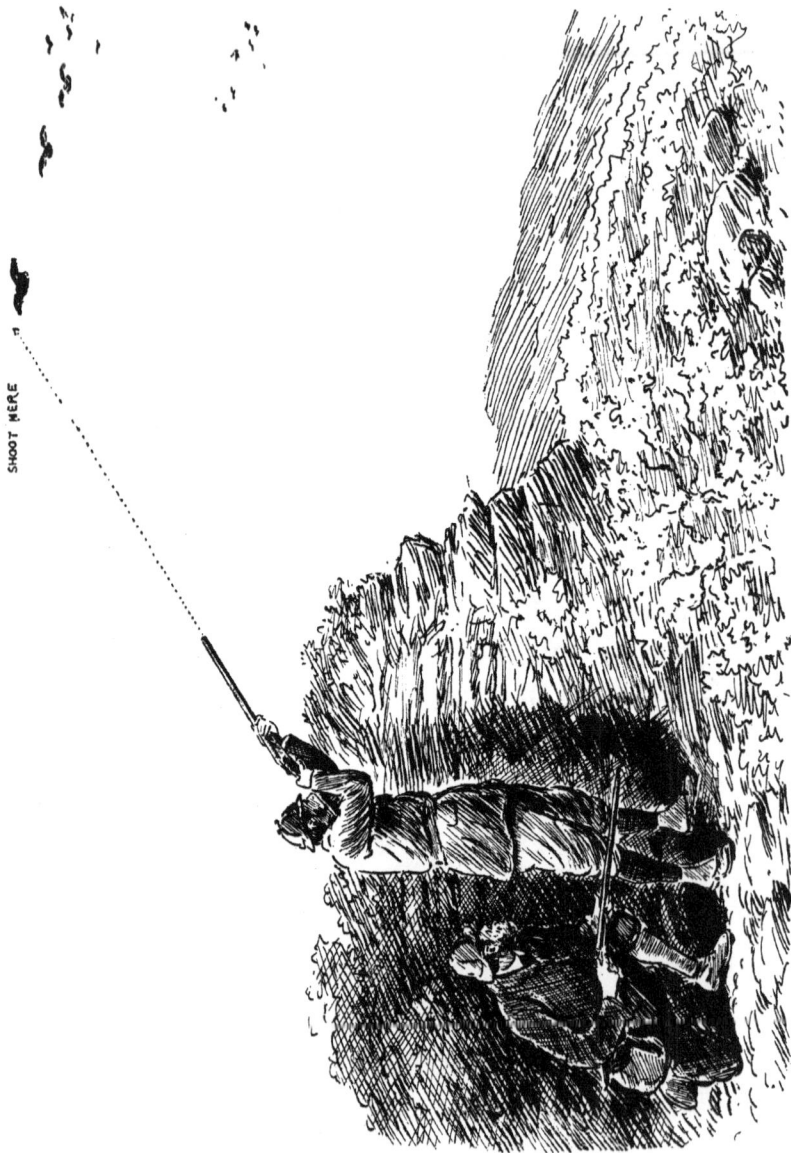

SHOOT HERE

No. 32]

The Approaching High Shot.

This Illustration (No. 33) is intended to show—1st, How an approaching Bird is to be taken; Secondly, How the same Bird is to be taken behind the Shooter after it has passed overhead, in each instance shooting in front, see page 77.

N.B.—Face completely round and then remount, see page 78.

SHOOT HERE

No. 34]

The Approaching Low Shot.

[72

The approaching low shot in partridge driving, where the hedge behind which the shooter is standing is lower than his shoulders, is really difficult, because the bird is often fired at when too far from the gun, or sometimes when much too near.

In shooting at an approaching low-flying bird, the shooter must get his gun well down and under the bird, or he will miss it by firing over—really behind it. Many birds are missed in this way owing to the fact that the gun is not brought enough up to the shoulder (*see Ill*. No. 34, page 72).

CRICKET.

··o◆o··

The following may be of interest to "Cricketing Shooters" :—
"SIR,—Lob Bowling is as dead as is Queen Anne, the reasons being quite plain. In the present fashionable over-arm bowling the ball leaves the bowler's hand at about the same height from the ground as is the batsman's eye ; hence during the first half of the ball's flight, the ball is but little affected by the energy of gravitation, and goes so straight to the batsman's eye that the latter knows but little of the pace of the ball, and therefore cannot form an early judgment of its length, that is, where it will pitch on the ground. Anyone accustomed to shooting young driven grouse from behind a wall will grasp my meaning. The grouse come skimming along, very low and straight at the gun, and the size or perspective of the bird is the only evidence of the speed and distance. If you fire when it is looking as big as a blackbird, you may kill nearly every shot, but miss that moment, and you will kill none. . . . . . —CHARLES ARMSTRONG."—*The Field*, 25th November, 1905.

To kill well that which is flying directly at the shooter's head, the bird should be covered by drawing a bead on it (*see Ill.* No. 35, page 75), and pulling at once, so as not to let the bird get too close.

SHOOT HERE.

The Approaching Direct Shot.

No. 35]

[75

SHOOT HERE.

Approached and Passed High Shot.

No 36]

[76

THE APPROACHED AND PASSED SHOT.

This kind of shooting often presents itself to the sportsman, especially in partridge driving, when the beaters are getting well up to the guns, so as to prevent the birds being shot at as they approach, lest a beater should be peppered.

If a bird flying high has to be shot after it has passed well overhead, the shooter must be careful to get well under the bird, or ahead of it, so as to prevent shooting behind. This is an easy shot and where one can look well over the gun, as long as the muzzle is thrown well under the bird, because the bird is never lost to view (*see Ill.* No. 36, page 76, also *Ill.* No. 33, page 71).

If a passed bird is flying low between the guns, the shooter must get well over or ahead of it. This is more difficult than the higher shot, as the bird is practically hidden by the gun, or, in other words, is flying under the line of sight (*see Ills*. Nos. 37 and 38, pages 79 and 80).

In turning to shoot at a bird after it has passed, be careful never to allow the gun to cover your neighbour, but take the gun down from the shoulder until *after* you have faced completely round, and then re-mount it (*see Ill*. No. 33, page 71).

No. 87]

Approached and Passed Low Shot (1)—A Quick Right.

SHOOT HERE!

No. 38]   [80

Approached and Passed (II) and useful Left.

No. 39]

Crossing—a Clean Right and Swinging Left.

G

SHOOT WELL
AHEAD

Crossing—" Hold well forward."

No. 40]

[82

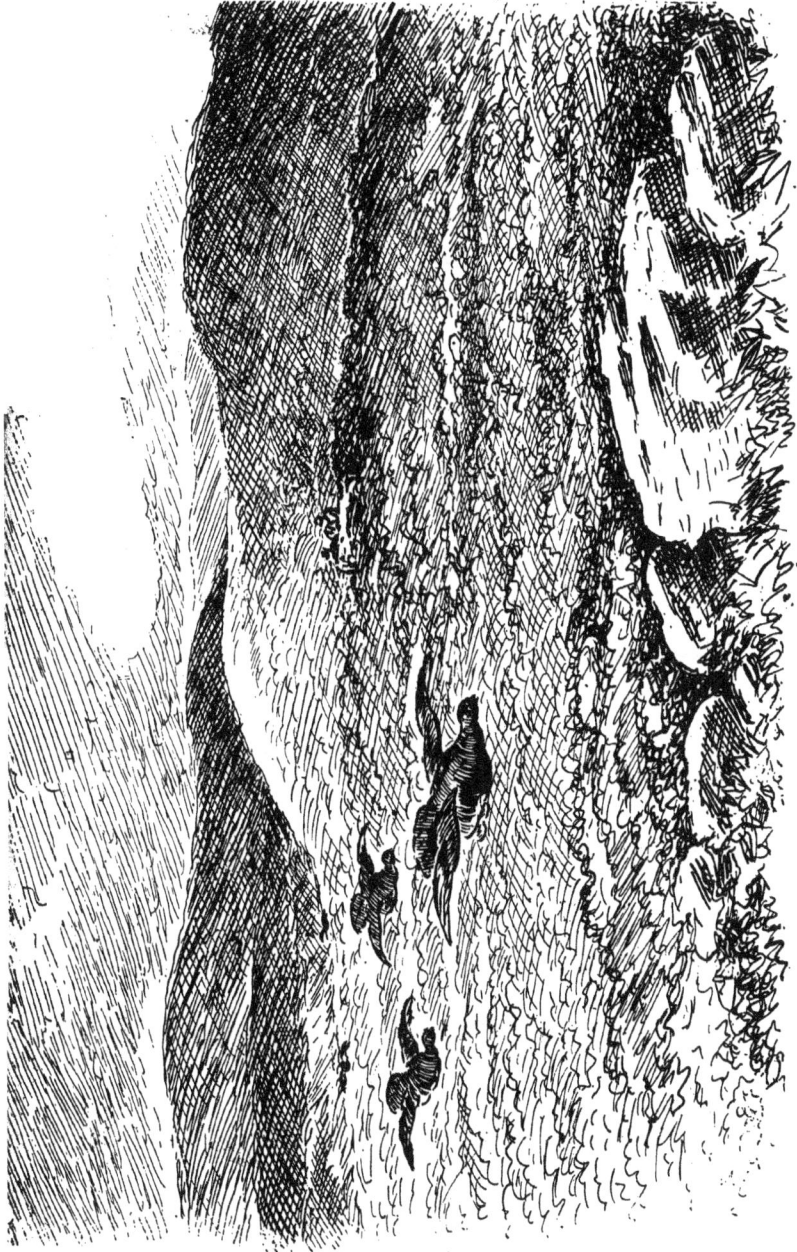

Driving—Crossing low Shot—" Hold well forward and low enough."

THE CROSSING SHOT.

These are generally easy shots; but the beginner must be careful to shoot only at his own birds, *i.e.*, those that really rise to him, and never shoot a bird that has crossed to the next-gun—whether to the right or left—unless he is an outside gun, when he can shoot well round (*see Ills.* Nos. 39 and 40).

In driving, crossing shots become more difficult, especially at driven grouse when flying low (*see Ill.* No. 41), as the tendency is to shoot very much over as well as behind—therefore bear in mind to get forward and well down to your bird, because of the trajectory of the shot, and also the fact that one is apt to give excessive elevation by keeping the eye too much above the breech of the gun.

To kill a bird cleanly and well if crossing to the right—generally the more difficult side—get well round, and, if necessary, move the left foot so as to bring the body far enough round, making the right foot the pivot. This will enable the balance of the body to be kept, and admit of the gun being swung ahead again for a second barrel, should the bird be missed with the first (*see Ill.* No. 42, page 86).

Crossing to the Right.

Crossing to the Left.

It is not always necessary to move the feet to turn to the left, as it is much easier to swing further and faster to the left than to the right (*see Ill.* No. **43**, page **87**).

The velocity or flight of a bird must be quickly judged—more in crossing shots than in any other; and an allowance of from three to even ten feet or more must be made, according to the pace of the bird and the distance it is away from the gun. At the longer distances the aim must also be a little over the bird, so as to allow it to be hit, as shot travels on a curve. More elevation is required when shooting up wind, than if shooting down wind.

Longer shots may be made at crossing than at straight-away birds; because shot strikes with greater force at a crossing object than at one which is flying in the same direction as the shot.

THE QUARTERING SHOT.

A quartering shot, as distinct from actual crossing shots, is very difficult; because, when a bird gets up, it may, more often than not, be flying at an oblique or obtuse angle. With these, very great practice is required to make a certain kill; because, besides the velocity of the flight of the bird, an allowance has also to be made on the lineal direction of the flying bird.

Care must be taken, with shots of this class, to hold the gun less in front than in actual crossing shots.

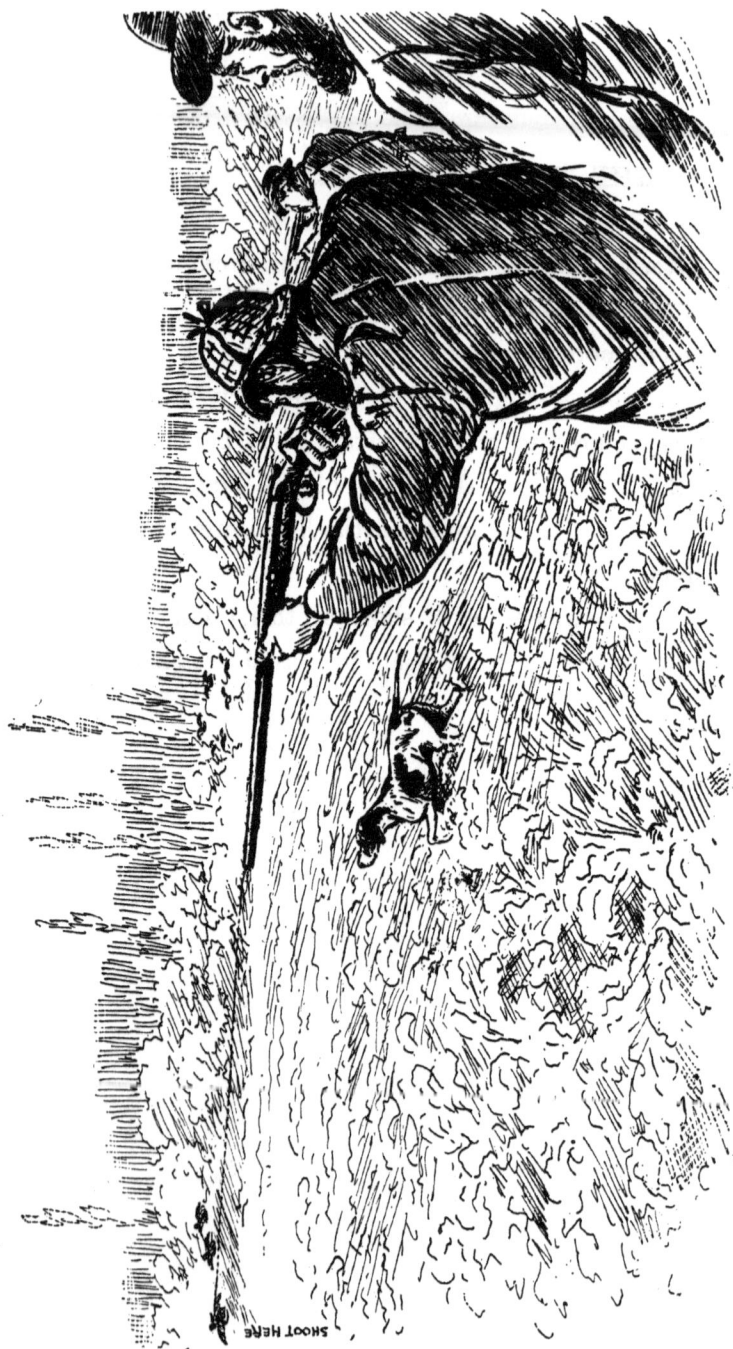

Straight-away Shot.

No. 44

SHOOT HERE

THE STRAIGHTFORWARD SHOT.

This class of shot may be considered under three headings—straight-away, high straight-away, and low straight-away shots.

As a rule, the sportsman has time to look well at his bird before putting the gun to his shoulder—especially in the early part of the season, when the covert is good and the birds lie well.

For the straight-away shot, where the bird flies in a bee-line, the gun should be put to the shoulder so as to be about in a line with the top of the back of the bird, if at a distance of 25 yards (*see Ill.* No. 44, page 90); but if at a greater distance, rather more above.

If a bird should fly straight, but having risen higher than the shooter, the gun should be mounted so as to be slightly under the bird (*see Ill.* No. 45, page 93).

High Straight-away Shot.

SHOOT HERE

No. 46]

SHOOT HERE.

Low Straight-away and Skimming.

[94

If a bird on rising flies very low—just skimming away—then the gun should be mounted so as to be well over or in advance of the bird (*see Ill.* No. 46, page 94); because in this class of shot the tendency is to wait too long before pulling the trigger, and then the bird is missed—owing to the shot striking where it was, rather than where the shooter intended it to be, according to his aim.

THE ASCENDING SHOT.

This is a difficult shot, because the general tendency is to shoot too much point-blank at the bird; whereas, when a bird ascends, it does so at a great pace, and the gun must therefore be mounted quickly, and be well over the bird to be struck (*see Ill*. No. 47, page 97).

The Ascending Shot—Shoot well over.

No. 47]

[97

H

Only Tailed.

A pheasant found amongst roots or in a hedge-row is almost invariably missed, because its flight is so different from that of other game—the bird often being shot in the tail feathers instead of in the body (*see Ill.* No. 48, page 98). Bear in mind, therefore, to shoot well over an ascending bird, and pull directly the gun is at the shoulder. A moment's delay is sure to cause a miss, to the chagrin of the shooter, who perhaps sees his bird going off with a leg down—if even that; more likely with only a few feathers gently settling to the ground.

THE DESCENDING SHOT.

More care is really required in making a clean kill at a descending bird than perhaps at any other; because, as a rule, these shots have to be made on the side of a mountain or hill, where the shooter has only space behind the bird—nothing, in fact, to assist him either in judging distance or pace. And it requires good judgment to determine at a moment that the gun must be so brought to the shoulder as to be slightly under the bird, if going straight away down hill (*see Ill.* No. 49, page 101); or, if to the right or left, slightly in advance—which tends to make the shot more difficult. At the same time, if good clean kills are obtained, nothing looks prettier, or establishes the reputation of the shooter as being a really first-class shot.

There are times when grouse in crossing a valley fly as shewn in (*Ill.* No. 50), they then present a somewhat similar shot to that of the low or straight-away one (*see Ill.* No. 46); but as there is nothing to assist the shooter to judge distance they are more difficult, and unless great quickness is shewn the bird is soon out of shot.

The Down-hill, or Descending Shot.

No. 49]

Low flying, and crossing a Valley.

No. 50]

Position for a Snap at a Cock,

THE SNAP SHOT.

Snap shots have frequently to be taken at snipe, woodcock, and ground game; and to be able to kill well, it is very essential that the gun should fit well, and mount at once to the shoulder for correct alignment. A snap shot can more easily be taken by leaning well forward, so that there is nothing to prevent the gun being brought well up to its place instantaneously—(*see Ill.* No. 51, page 103). A man who looks along his gun can never be as good a snap shot as the one who shoots entirely with his eyes fixed on the object he desires to kill. A snap shot may often cause a miss; but what can make up for the delight of a kill when snapping at a woodcock? Nothing in my humble estimation.

SHOOTING HARES.

Hares are gradually becoming extinct; and in the face of the possibility of offending some of my readers, I must frankly say that I think hares should never be shot where it is so, but should be left for those who prefer the sport of hunting and coursing. However, no doubt some of my readers would like to know what to do, in the event of their wishing to shoot them.

Hares travel at a great pace, and, although a large mark, they are very often missed—or rather wounded—and get away to die in a ditch or covert.

To kill a hare clean and well, if running away, the gun should be held well over it (*see Ill.* No. 52, page 106), so as to prevent hitting it in the hind quarters only.

Hold well forward,

SHOT HERE

No. 52]

SHOOT HERE!

Hold well inside

If coming towards the " gun " the aim should be well in front (*see Ill.* No. 53, page 107), and if running across to left or right, the aim or gun must be taken well in advance—sometimes as much as 6 ft.— especially if it has a clear run up a drain or furrow.

A hare should never be shot at at a greater distance than 35 to 40 yards, especially if going straight away.

Hares lie out in wheat, stubbles, fallows, clover and grass lands ; and if you find them in their form, give them time to get a fair distance before firing, as you are more likely to kill, and less likely to damage, than by shooting at such close quarters.

Where hares are likely to be found, the shooter should be very quiet ; because they are very shy, and often steal off and away at the sound of the voice or the closing of a gate.

SHOOTING RABBITS.

This is always good fun, and splendid practice for the beginner, because it teaches him to keep a good look-out, and handle or mount a gun quickly.

Rabbits, as a rule, only give time for a short sight of them. When bolting across a ride, always bear in mind to shoot where they are running to, and not where they are when you first see them (*see Ill.* No. 54, page 110).

Rabbit shooting in rough grass land, or in fern or furze, is capital sport, if with the assistance of beaters. A perfect line with the guns should be kept, so as to allow of the shooting to be made either forward, or at one that may break back and get through the line.

A good hedgerow will sometimes hold a great number of rabbits; and a spaniel or terrier working them, with a gun on either side of the hedge, is good sport at certain seasons—December and January for choice. Great care must be exercised in this sport, so as to avoid shooting or wounding the dogs, or perhaps your friend. Remember, as a golden rule, never to shoot at a rabbit on the top of a hedge bank,

Not where he is, but where he is bolting to.

A Quick Right and Left.

No 55]

[111

and on no account be led into shooting into or through a hedge, but let the rabbit be clear and going forward, or back along the outer edge of the ditch, well out in the field. Keep whistling to the "gun" with you, so that you may be opposite each other; and never shoot at a pheasant or any other bird that may be put up, if it is crossing to your friend's side of the hedge, but let him shoot when the object has got over and clear; simply call to him that something is crossing to his side, so that he may be ready for it.

Rabbits are generally found lying out in tufts of grass in fine weather, and, when started, are certain to make for the hedge or covert (*see Ill.* No. 55, page 111). To make sure of killing them, get well ahead, and shoot at the first chance, because a second is seldom given.

Rabbits are sometimes killed with small bore rifles, built for the purpose; but, although this may be good amusement, it is not nearly such profitable practice for the beginner as shooting them with a gun.

NOTE.—Charles Lancaster supplies a Switchback Rabbit (travelling about 18 yards) which is excellent practice for ground game shooting, and affords a certain amount of amusement on an " off " day.

THE "POT" OR SITTING SHOT.

How annoying it is to shoot at an object, such as a crouching wounded bird or a sitting rabbit, that will not move—thus necessitating a "pot" shot—and to find that, even after a considerable amount of preparation, the object fired at has not been touched at all, perhaps even after a second barrel has been discharged.

I have frequently heard the remark, "Oh! you shoot it, So-and-so; I can't hit anything sitting. Make it run or move, and I'm your man." Why is this? Surely it cannot be difficult to shoot at an object perfectly still.

I think the reason is this: Very few sportsmen have so studied the question as to know that all shot travels curvilinearly. They are ignorant of the exact point-blank range of their gun; and they are not aware that with large shot, such as No. 5, the trajectory curve is flatter than with smaller shot, such as No. 7, and that, consequently, if they kill with one aim, with shot of one size, a different aim must be taken for the other. Yet these are facts, not surmises, and have been proved by actual experiment.

Preparing for a "Pot" Shot.

"SHOOT HERE"

A Sitting or " Pot " Shot

No. 57]

[115

Therefore, at or inside the point-blank range of the gun, and with one known load, by shooting just at the angle formed at the point when the sportsman can see the ground and the object on it (*see Ill.* No. 57, page 115), a kill is a certainty ; whereas at a longer distance the gun must be held above the point of the first aim—sometimes quite over the object to be struck—the shape of the ground being noticed, as to whether the shooting is on the level, or up or down hill.

It is useful to make this experiment on a road or path where the shot-marks are clearly visible, by shooting at a turnip, root, or even old tennis ball.

We can thus understand why, with modern Express Rifles, with flat trajectory, more kills are scored than with the old-fashioned ones, where the trajectory, or curve, was very great—thereby causing the bullet to go over or under, according to the point-blank range and the error in sighting or judging of distance by the shooter.

MISSING.

A chief cause of missing birds on the wing is the fault of shooting below the object aimed at—the gun not being kept up enough. You must aim above straightforward shots (unless a gun is very straight or too long in the stock), and well ahead or in advance of crossing ones (*see Ill.* No. 39, page 81). There is little fear of shooting too high, or too far in front, if the gun is well brought up to the shoulder; the aim is always too low and too point-blank at first. A sportsman frequently kills much better with his second barrel than with his first, because he instinctively swings his gun further ahead, or raises it over the object to be shot; and also because the hand or trigger-finger obeys the eye quicker, without that perceptible pause which is so fatal to all good shooting. In drawing or pulling the trigger, care should be taken to do it entirely with the finger, and not with any motion of the hand; or the tendency will be to pull off, in some cases to the right, but often to the left, owing to the gun being pulled across by the extra leverage of the left arm and hand.

When you miss, try and think why you miss; and if you steadfastly keep both eyes open, it will assist you in finding out the cause. If you cannot ascertain the reason, owing to the flinching or closing of the eyes from the noise the report of the gun gives, put an exploded cartridge into the gun, cover the next bird carefully, then swing the gun and pull the trigger instantaneously. This will enable you to see whether the fault was owing to the gun not being exactly where you wished it at the moment of pulling the trigger. Try this several times in the field, and it will help you considerably. If shooting in company, walk or stand close to one of the party, and make the experiment.

This test may be made quietly and by oneself at larks, blackbirds, and even sparrows, without much trouble or fear of disturbing game, as plenty of these birds may be found; but be careful not to mount the gun at them too soon. Be deliberate, and wait until they have reached a fair range; this will greatly assist in lessening that flush or snap shooting which is so difficult for young sportsmen to overcome. I mean that uncomfortable surprised feeling which puts one off when partridges rise with a whirr, but which never troubles or interferes with a good steady old sportsman, who gives his game plenty of grace, at the same time is pretty certain of getting a right-and-left out of most rises.

Never fire at a bird too near; because, if a kill is made, the game is so dreadfully mangled as not to be worth picking up. And never shoot at too long a range, as the tendency is to wound; and a bird so struck is seldom recovered, but gets away to die a lingering death. Such shooting is most unsportsmanlike and cruel.

"SHOOTING WITH A PAIR OF GUNS."

Although previously this Treatise has been specially a primer rather than a work embracing all and every phase of instruction necessary, I have been requested by many of my patrons to include, at the first available opportunity, a few lines about "Shooting with a Pair of Guns and a Loader," therefore the illustrations, Nos. 58, 59, and 60, pages 121 and 123, will give a good idea of what is required.

For choice, the loader should stand just behind the right-hand shoulder facing the same direction as the "gun" (*see Ill.* No. 58, page 121). He should be well prepared with a stock of cartridges conveniently carried in a bag, with an assistant having a further supply for replenishing his own bag between "drives."

The gun he is holding should be with muzzles up and slightly sloped to the left. After his "gun" has fired either one or both barrels, the loader should be ready to take the gun (from him) with the left hand, passing the second gun, which he has had loaded in readiness, with the right hand holding the small part of the stock only, and taking the fired gun with the left hand by the barrels, and the "gun" should take the loaded gun from the loader also with his left hand. The drill practically being to each "take with the left hand" (*see Ill.* No. 59, page 121).

The "gun" should at all times, before handing his gun to the loader, pull the "safety slide" back, so

SHOOTING WITH A PAIR OF GUNS.

that the word "**SAFE**" is exposed, the loader having nothing to do with it. Should the "gun" forget to do this, I would respectfully suggest that the loader warn him that he has not done so ; otherwise, should only one barrel be fired, he would be passing back to the loader a gun loaded in one barrel, and at full cock, a *very* dangerous proceeding.

The loader, on receiving the gun, should face sufficiently to the rear, turning the barrels well away from the shooting line to prevent anyone being covered in the act of opening the gun for the fired cases to be removed, or while re-loading, and should not face about until the gun is properly closed, then see that the barrels are pointing upwards, and held as in the original position (*see Ill*. No. 58, page 121).

After each "stand" or "drive" the loader should remove all cartridges from the barrels (*see Ill*. No. 61, page 127), and not re-load until his "gun" has arrived at the next "stand" or position.

N.B.—I would suggest that a loader should have with him a Cartridge Extractor, of the spring clip or universal pattern, a knife, a small strap, and some string.

No. 60]

SHOOTING WITH A PAIR OF GUNS.

[123

THE MOST DIFFICULT SHOTS.

From *The Badminton Magazine*, September, 1905.

We have all heard times out of number that he who wishes to put his shooting skill to a fair test may advantageously bestow some attention on the elusive, twisting snipe or repair to the yawning seaside caverns where the blue rock pigeons are quartered in solid battalions. The question of the most difficult shots to take forms the subject of an interesting article appearing in a London magazine in which are quoted the views of the most expert manipulators of the shot-gun. The Earl de Grey, who is admittedly the finest game shot in the kingdom, declares that the high pheasant flying with the wind with a drop and a curl towards the gunner is the bird that has the best chance of avoiding the shower of lead. Lord Walsingham, who holds the record for a single day's bag of grouse, experiences the greatest trouble in bringing down a game-bird that passes straight over his head and that must be shot by turning round and firing at it as it flies away. The low partridge or pheasant on his left puts Major Acland-Hood in the greatest quandary, and the Marquis of Granby is most disturbed by a pheasant sailing along with perfectly motionless wings. The dropping "long-tail" with steady wings is the most perplexing mark that Lord Ashburton encounters, and Lord Westbury and the Hon. Henry Stoner hold similar opinions. Prince Victor Duleep Singh is always greatly nonplussed by a high dropping pheasant approaching with the wind over tall trees and the guns in a valley; and the Hon. A. E. Gathorne-Hardy, author of that delightful book, "Autumns in Argyllshire," affirms that the bird most readily missed is the pheasant coming straight at the gunner too low to take in front, and which he strives to dispose of by turning round and firing at it as it recedes in the distance. The general consensus of opinion undoubtedly is that the denizens of the covert under certain conditions are the game-birds most difficult to bag.—*The Scottish Field,* January, 1906.

A WORD OF ADVICE FOR ALL.

Always look upon a gun as a death-dealing weapon. Therefore, at all times be careful in which direction it is pointed, so as to avoid any possibility of its being in line or " laid on " to anybody or any animal whose life you would not like to take (*see Ills.* Nos. 23, 20 and 24 ; pages 57, 54 and 58).

Accidents easily happen ; therefore, whether loaded or unloaded, always exercise the greatest amount of caution in the handling of gun, rifle, pistol or revolver.

If the above simple words are remembered, there can be no excuse whatever in the mere saying " I was not aware it was loaded," after mischief has been done.

I once read the last words of a suicide, in which he stated he hoped the jury would not return a verdict of " accidental death " or " death by misadventure," because he thoroughly understood what he was doing at the time he shot himself, and did not wish it handed down to posterity that he belonged to the class of idiots who inadvertently handle a weapon at a risk to themselves or others.

ANGLEY PARK
Shooting Regulations.

1. Any shooter convicted of letting off his gun accidentally to be fined 10s., and to incur the same penalty if the said offence be committed by his loader.

2. The owner of any gun found loaded during lunch, or at any other time, out of his own hands, or his loader's, to be fined 5s.

3. Any shooter convicted of pointing his gun, loaded, or unloaded, at any person whatever, to be fined 2s. 6d., and to incur the same penalty if the said offence be committed by his loader.

4. Any shooter convicted of getting over any fence, gate or ditch, without extracting cartridges, or handing his gun at half-cock, or bolted, to a bystander, to be fined 2s. 6d., and to incur the same penalty if the said offence be committed by his loader.

5. Any shooter convicted of plastering a pheasant going a more sporting shot to another gun, to be fined 1s.

6. Any shooter convicted of wilfully shooting another man's bird, to be fined 1s.

7. Guns with the beaters are requested not to fire at birds going straight forward.

8. Guns are reminded that it is seldom safe to fire at a bird in covert unless the sky can be seen behind it.

9. Any gun bagging a woodcock to receive 2s. 6d. from each other gun.

N.B.—FINES WILL GO TO THE KEEPERS.

(By kind permission of Edward L. Tomlin, Esq., Angley Park, Cranbrook, Kent.)

Extracting Cartridges before getting over a fence,
N.B.—This should always be done.

PART II.

The previous pages of this work treat of the practical part of the Art of Shooting, so far as regards the means which the sportsman should adopt, under the varying conditions of the bird's flight, to use his gun with effect. Now it is proposed to devote some further space to remarks on the gun and its accessories, and matters of a more or less theoretical character; and one of the first among the subjects to be taken into consideration will be that of

CLOTHES.

In looking round at those about to join in a day's shooting, it does not take long for the practised eye to detect which are the sportsmen and which are the tailor's models. It is simply astonishing at times to imagine where some of the materials, with their rainbow colours and mixtures, are designed and made.

Clothing should be so chosen as to resemble, as much as possible, in tone and colour, the surround ings where the shooting or sport is to be had.

Clothes should be cut so as to fit well, but at the same time permit of the sportsman being able to handle his gun freely in almost any position, and not to impede his movements. Badly-cut clothes, too tight across the back or in the sleeves, often prevent a man shooting well.

The softer the material the better; and a well-cut Norfolk jacket, and loosely-cut breeches or knicker-bockers, with warm underclothing*, are the best for sport generally. Good boots, in which the feet are perfectly comfortable, are most essential; as I defy any man to shoot well or enjoy his day, if his feet are galled or blistered. Never start a walk on the hills or fields in new boots—it has been done very often, but usually with most saddening results.

A warm light cape or cloak is a very useful adjunct to the sportsman's outfit (*see Ills.* No. 62 and 63). One that is easily rolled up and carried in a sling at the back, or by an attendant, forms a comfortable wrap in bad weather, or a seat, or cushion to kneel on in the event of a rest being required; and is as much protection as an extra coat in a long drive home.

* I specially advise the use of Dr. Jaeger's Pure Wool Clothing. [See footnote, page 134.]

No. 62]

A useful Cloak for a long wait.

[130

No. 63]

A Cloak that can be thrown back for a Snap Shot.

[131

No. 64]　　　　In Covert—"The Lancaster Smock."　　　　[132

No 65]　　　　　**In the Butt—"The Lancaster Smock."**　　　　　[133

A close-fitting cap should be worn, with peaks at
the back and front to protect the eyes and throw off
the wet. Care should be taken in selecting the
colour, as the covering of the head is seen first by
birds in driving; and, if too conspicuous, it will
turn them from you.

NOTE.—Since the publication of the previous editions, the
matter of protection from rough weather has secured my
further attention with great success, as will be seen from the
following letter which appeared in the *Field* of the 28th
November, 1891, and (*Ills.* 64 and 65) :—

" I have now a garment which will keep out the heaviest of rains, even
if driven by a gale; and at the same time I am able to get a 'right and
left' either from a 'butt,' field of roots, or covert side without let or
hindrance. I feel sure that many will welcome this useful addition to
their sporting kit, as I consider it just as useful to a yatchsman or an angler
as to a 'gunner.' The material is perfectly waterproof, yet not in the
least airproof, as you can both breathe and smoke through it ; and the
Smock does not cause perspiration. as, being cut ' full,' plenty of room is
given for ventilation.

" CHARLES LANCASTER."

GUN CLEANING.

I always make a point of seeing after the cleaning of my own guns when away shooting, and I find the following the best plan :—

Never attempt to clean your gun over-night, if the time is too short to do it properly, because often one is tempted to leave it after giving it only a temporary clean; whereas, if left till the next morning, it receives thorough attention.

I find the best way to remove all leading, fouling, and general dirt after a day's shooting is the following : Screw the jag on to the cleaning rod, and then put just as much dry tow or small squares of clean rag on it as will enter the barrel fairly tight. Do not put any oil at all this time, as the absence of oil enables the dry tow or rag to grip the dirt well, and removes it very quickly if the rod is passed from breech to muzzle briskly a few times. After doing this, look through the barrel to see if clean; if not, continue the operation a little longer, and if necessary increase the amount of tow or rag to make it fit the barrel tighter; then take some clean tow or rag, and apply a mixture of vaseline and sperm oil—or either alone will do—and again pass the rod up and down the barrel quickly once or twice ; then, for the last time, put a little more oil on the rag, and pass it through to the muzzle, and back, slowly, so as to deposit as much of the oil as will remain. The gun should always be looked at two or three days after it has been shot with, to see that no dirt has been left.

In wiping out the barrels, the muzzles should never be placed on a stone or concrete floor, but on a soft piece of wood.

On no account use a wire brush for the barrels, as such brushes do more harm than good.

If the gun has been out in the wet or snow, it should be well wiped over with a soft rag the same evening, and not be allowed to remain till the morning.

It is best to send guns to their makers, or to some practical maker, at the end of each season, certainly before the next commences, to see if all is in order. If this were done more frequently, much inconvenience and annoyance would be saved to the shooter.

The strikers should frequently be taken out, wiped clean and dry, a little vaseline applied, and then replaced; a dirty clogged-up striker often retards the ignition of the charge, and sometimes causes a miss-fire, or, which is much more serious, an accidental discharge when in the act of closing the gun.

The great .fault is putting too much oil on a gun, so that it often gets gummy, or clogs the working of a gun, more especially "hammerless" and "ejectors." Vaseline, well worked on and into a soft piece of rag or an old pocket-handkerchief, is the best thing for cleaning all the outside parts of a gun, such as outsides of barrels (after the insides have been carefully wiped out), lock-plates, breech-action, triggers and guard, and other parts of metal that are exposed. *Never* allow oil to be applied by a feather, or any brush that is likely to do so too liberally.

Should the locks or any other of the interior working parts become dry, the smallest quantity possible of watchmakers' or any other highly-refined oil may be applied with a needle dipped in it—care being taken to wipe off any that appears superfluous; this will prevent the parts so treated from becoming sticky or clogged.

MEASURING A GUN.

This method has been used by many authors, but the best and simplest description I have seen is that in " The Dead Shot," so I copy the wording :—" Take a shoulder gun as near your fit as you can, and fasten tightly with twine a perfectly straight spline of wood, edgewise, along the groove of the rib which divides the barrels, leaving the breech end of the spline projecting over, and just beyond the heel of the gun-stock, as shown in the illustration; then lay the gun upon a table and measure with careful precision to the 16th of an inch as follows :—

For the bend of stock—from G to H, and from E to F.

For the length of stock—from A to B, A to C, A to D.

The three latter measurements being taken from the fore-trigger to the edge of the heel of the gun-stock."

The amount of " cast-off "—*i.e.*, the set of the stock towards the shoulder, so as to get the perfect alignment along the rib of the barrels required by each individual, whether using the right or left eye—is very essential. Much correspondence has taken place in the *Field*, etc., on this subject; but I consider the best method, and one I have carried out for some years, is so clearly put by that well-known Sportsman " One who has Fired some 20,000 Trial Shots at Marks," in his letter which appeared in the *Field* of Jan. 5th, 1889, that I reproduce the same :—

Sir,—A great deal has lately appeared in your columns on this subject, and doubtless where the sportsman is not sufficiently up, practically, in the gun to determine this for himself, it is about the most difficult point the gun-maker has to deal with. I may here mention a plan which, under certain conditions, never fails, and was that by which I determined the amount of crook I required when I had to use cross-eyed guns, when my right eye first failed me. The conditions are where a man shuts one eye and squints down the barrel, or where he has but one eye and the other is so weak that one does all the work in shooting. Shut a piece of thin writing paper into the breech of a gun so as to stand up about half-an-inch, then proceed to cut an extremely narrow V just over the exact centre of the break-off. If, on throwing the gun up, the

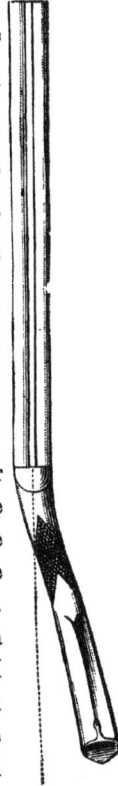

shooter finds this narrow V occupied by the sight on the muzzle, all is right; if not, by carefully raising the head without laterally shifting its position, it will easily be seen on which side of the V the sight comes; then cut away the paper on that side until the sight just shows itself on pitching the gun to the shoulder. This distance being added to or deducted from the cast-off already in the gunstock, the exact cast-off required will be found. I have not the smallest doubt that if many men who are in the habit of missing systematically would try this experiment, the reason of their doing so would become apparent.

ONE WHO HAS FIRED SOME 20,000 TRIAL SHOTS AT MARKS.

Brighton.

The Author has a measuring gun specially designed, so as to get, in a moment, the exact amount of cast-off required by any sportsman.*

At the same time it may be advisable to state, in addition, the height of the shooter; and if he possesses any peculiarities of figure—as short neck or long neck, slender figure or very stout—they should be mentioned.

The length of barrels required should also be indicated, and if the boring is to be Cylinder or "Non-Choke" for both, or Modified or Full Choke.

[* See footnote, page 15.]

CAST-OFF.

During a long correspondence on this subject, I published the following letter in the *Field* of the 17th November, 1888 :—

Sir,—In reply to your correspondent " Amateur," cast-off should be given to all guns intended to be used from the right shoulder ; cast-on for all guns to be used from the left shoulder. A gun-maker must make a study of this important feature in gun-making, or he can never make a perfect " fitter." I maintain that unless a gun, to be used from right shoulder and right eye, is cast-off according to the figure of the gentleman one is building for (it may be only one-eighth of an inch, or it may be as much or more than five-eighths), and unless this cast-off is given, the gun will lie across the body—*i.e.*, point to the left and shoot to the left. So will it shoot to the left if the stock is so long that the gun mounts on the arm instead of the pectoral muscle. This may be corrected sometimes by laying the head over to the right, but that is a move after the gun has been put to the shoulder, and is fatal to good shooting.

To prove that my statements are correct, I ask you to come to my private shooting grounds and witness the shooting of guns with more or less cast-off at a target.

Only last week a gentleman brought me a gun, by another maker, with a cast-off of 1½ inches (supposed to be enough for a left-eyed gun, whereas it would have required a cast-off between 3 inches and 4 inches). This gentleman was really left-eyed, but, as he always closed that eye, he was, in fact, right-eyed when putting a gun to his shoulder; and, to demonstrate how perfectly wrong his gun was stocked, by shooting quickly at a plate, he found he could not hit it at all, although it was 6 ft. by 4 ft., the centre of the pattern made by the gun being found about 5 ft. to the right of the point he was looking at with his right eye, and expecting to cover and hit. I changed his gun to one with a cast-off of ¼-inch, and he covered the point he shot at every time.

Now, I ask, what chance had he of hitting anything at all in a day's shooting, except, perhaps, by " shooting at the cock and killing the crow ? " Yet this gun was made for him by a maker who had taken a lot of pains to measure his customer for it. Is it to be wondered at that your correspondents write that " gun-makers do not know as much as they claim to ? "

If any gentlemen wish to test the accuracy of my statements, if they will pay me a visit I will let them handle my specially designed gun for measuring, and will show them in a few minutes the effect of " cast-off " and " cast-on " in alignment.

CHARLES LANCASTER.

I have seen this in many cases, and those to whom I have explained it have seen it very clearly, and, at my special suggestion, have either shot with the left eye closed, *before putting the gun to the shoulder*, or else have allowed me to make them a cross-eyed gun— in other words, a gun built to fit the right shoulder, but cast off sufficiently to allow the rib of the barrels to come opposite to the left eye for the alignment; and I am pleased to say that, after a little trouble and practice, they have found their shooting vastly improved, much to the astonishment of their friends and themselves.

I am convinced in my own mind, from the most careful noting of this fact during my experience of coaching and fitting, that, from the peculiarity of vision indicated, a man may unconsciously be most dangerous at the covert side, because he often " shoots at the cock and kills the crow." Where covert is thick, with trees having smooth bark, such as beech, birch, &c., he may, as he thinks, be shooting between two trees, whereas his faulty sight causes him really to point the gun more to the left-hand one, whereby the shot is liable to *ricochet* from it to his next hand " gun," who may unfortunately receive some of the glancing pellets in his face, or perhaps lose an eye. The offender will all the while protest that such a result is impossible, because he shot at an object a good deal to the right of the tree, or *vice versa*, should he be a left-handed shot ; but it is nevertheless a fact. If any one doubts the truth of this assertion, let him cover up or shut the right eye, keep the head fairly erect, and take a snap shot at a mark on a white-washed wall, and see where the shot will go ; or let him make the experiment when standing in front of a looking-glass, and he will find the muzzles of the barrels pointing all away to the left. In other words, he will find the left eye, and the bead on the barrels, aligned a long way to the left side of his face, as reflected accurately by the glass (*see Ill.* No. 3).

[* See footnotes, page 20.]

MODERN METHODS OF SHOOTING.

From the *Field*, October 21st, 1905.

If one of those good old sportsmen who flourished fifty or a hundred years ago were to rise from his grave and witness the performance of some of our modern gunners, he would probably receive a considerable shock. Modern methods of shooting would doubtless surprise him, while nothing probably would seem stranger than the details involved in the choice of a gun and learning how to shoot with it. Our forefathers knew nothing of the modern machinery of gun-fitting, nor of the paraphernalia of the shooting school, at which the learner is taught the first principles of marksmanship. One can imagine a shooter of the old school picking up a try-gun—that wonderfully ingenious contrivance of the latter-day gunmaker designed to insure a perfect fit, no matter what the peculiarities of build or eyesight may be. He would marvel as he watched the tyro being instructed by the expert in charge of the gunmaker's shooting range. How surprised he would be to see the duffer, who at the outset could hardly hit a haystack, brought round by degrees until he could place the charge time after time in the correct place, and break both the artificial rising bird and the crossing bird sent swiftly athwart the horizontal whitewashed plate. After that the trap would be brought into use, and imitation driven birds sent at varying speeds over the head of the shooter. One could not have a better representation of live partridges and pheasants, the latter shot over one's head from a tower 60 feet high, and the man who can "kill" repeatedly six out of seven of these fast-flying clay birds will figure as no mean performer in field and covert.

There are those, of course, who scoff at the modern methods of gun-fitting, and would try to persuade you that it is all nonsense. They tell you that our forefathers managed to shoot without any such contrivances, and that we ought to be able to do the same. But our forefathers indulged in a much easier form of shooting than that which is now in vogue, and they, therefore, did not need the aids to quick and difficult shooting which to-day are found necessary to develop a crack shot.

We drive our partridges to-day, and shoot them as they pass high overhead, often with a strong wind behind them, and on modern shootings, when well managed, the majority of the pheasants killed are real rocketers, towering high above the tops of the woods from which they are driven. It requires a good man, one who has had plenty of practice, to bring down such birds with any consistency.

It must be admitted, of course, that all the best appliances in the world are useless without the advice of an expert who knows how to use them and how to instruct the beginner in the way he should go. Learners are of three kinds—the youthful tyro, the man who has taken up shooting late in life, and the man who has had some amount of shooting, and is not satisfied with his performance in the field. The first is, naturally, the easiest to teach, and unless he is a born duffer may be made an apt pupil in a very short time. The second type, being of more mature years, probably has ideas of his own, which are not always correct, and these have to be eradicated before he can make a proper beginning. The last mentioned, as a rule, is the most difficult of all to deal with. One has not only to teach him what he should do to improve, but also what he should leave off doing. He has in the course of his shooting career learned many bad habits, and these he must unlearn before he can make a start. But whether your pupil be the inexperienced youth, the would-be middle-aged sportsman, or the dissatisfied shooter, it will be a strange thing if you cannot improve his marksmanship to some degree after a course of lessons at the school, even if you cannot make of him the expert that you would wish. There are, of course, some men who, do what they will and try as they may, will never shoot well, and no one can teach them, for they have no aptitude to learn. There are others who, because of some physical infirmity, can never become brilliant performers, although as regards this class of shooters circumstances may sometimes be so adapted as to make them eventually fairly good shots.

EAST SUSSEX.

FOUR-BARRELLED GUNS.

The only one known was that manufactured by Charles Lancaster, Panton Street, Haymarket.

The earlier models were objected to owing to the " pull off " being dependent on a drawing or long pull of the trigger. In the later model the pulls are similar to those of an ordinary gun, consequently removing the cause for objection.

Sir Ralph Payne Gallwey, Bart., having used one, grouse driving, wrote as follows :—

" I used the four-barrelled gun the other day grouse driving. I consider it admirable both in theory and practice, and most useful as a third gun for packs coming over, as by its means four birds can then be shot without taking the gun from the shoulder. It can also, in such cases, be fired much faster than can two double barrels, however quickly the latter may be changed and loaded. As a second gun on moors, where only two guns are required, it would be especially convenient. I do not see why it should be thought any more unsportsmanlike to use a gun with four barrels for game, such as driven grouse flying past in hundreds, than to use a pair of guns with two barrels each. I was pleased to find the new gun similar to an ordinary one as to weight, handling, pull of triggers, etc., and that it is, besides, so easy of manipulation."

N.B.—Rifles have been made on the same model.

HAMMER OR HAMMERLESS GUNS.

Hammerless guns have come into favour with the generality of sportsmen, but a purchaser should insist upon having the "blocking or intercepting safeties" in his gun, as well as the usual locking safety bolt for the triggers. The "automatic" trigger safety bolt should be selected rather than an independent one, especially where two or more guns may be used,—the services of a loader being necessary. The automatic bolt effectually locks the triggers, and thereby prevents the accidental discharge of the gun from the loader carelessly touching or pulling the trigger when handling or unloading the gun. When shooting with two or more guns with a "loader," after firing one or more barrels the "safety slide" should always be put to "**SAFE**" before handing the gun back to the "loader" (*see Ills.* Nos. 58, 59, and 60, pages 121 and 123.)

Those who have witnessed a heavy day's driving or covert shooting, where two or more guns are used, can well testify to the absolute necessity of this.

CARTRIDGE EJECTING GUNS,

WHICH EJECT ONLY THE FIRED CARTRIDGE.

(See Ills. Nos. 66 and 67.)

These guns have now superseded all others.

The cartridges covered partly or wholly with brass, or having waterproof tubes, such as " Pegamoid," " Kynoid " or " Bonnaud," are better adapted for these guns—because in wet or damp weather they are less liable to be affected, consequently they give the ejectors less work to do than if the ordinary paper cartridges are used.

N.B.—CHARLES LANCASTER's latest Ejector Guns are made with two parts only, viz., the ejecting hammer and the mainspring both in the fore-end, as illustrated.

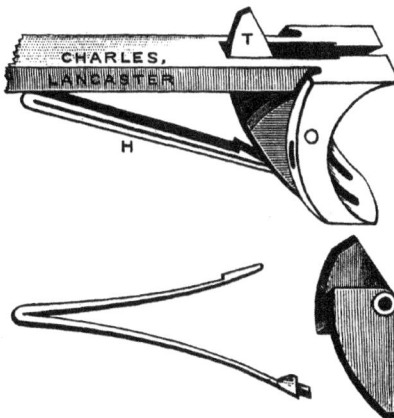

Charles Lancaster's Two-part or "H.T." Ejector.

A MODERN GUN.

(1889.)

The following letter appeared in *The Field*, and still expresses my opinion:—

SIR,—Your correspondent X, in your issue of the 1st inst., asks for some ideas respecting a really serviceable game gun, as it might assist him and others to arrive at a conclusion, and thereby get what they want. I therefore beg to give him mine, and hope they will be of some service.

I say, first, that a sportsman should put himself into the hands of a thoroughly practical man, and find out what weight and bore of gun would be best suited to his special requirements; then be properly measured, so as to ensure the gun fitting him, as so much depends thereon.

I agree with him, that a pattern of, say, for the first barrel 140 to 150, and for the other 150 to 160—not a bunching pattern, but one that is fairly and evenly distributed over the usual 30 in. circle or more—would be best, if of 12-bore. A pattern that only covers about 20 in. very closely, and then leaves the remainder very patchy and irregular, is bad; as to shoot well with a gun that shows a close centre, a man must be a better performer than the average shot.

Cartridges should be loaded with the best materials, and I consider it a decided advantage always to use one uniform load, so that one's judgment is not liable to be handicapped owing to being upset by an unknown quantity in the shooting of irregularly performing cartridges.

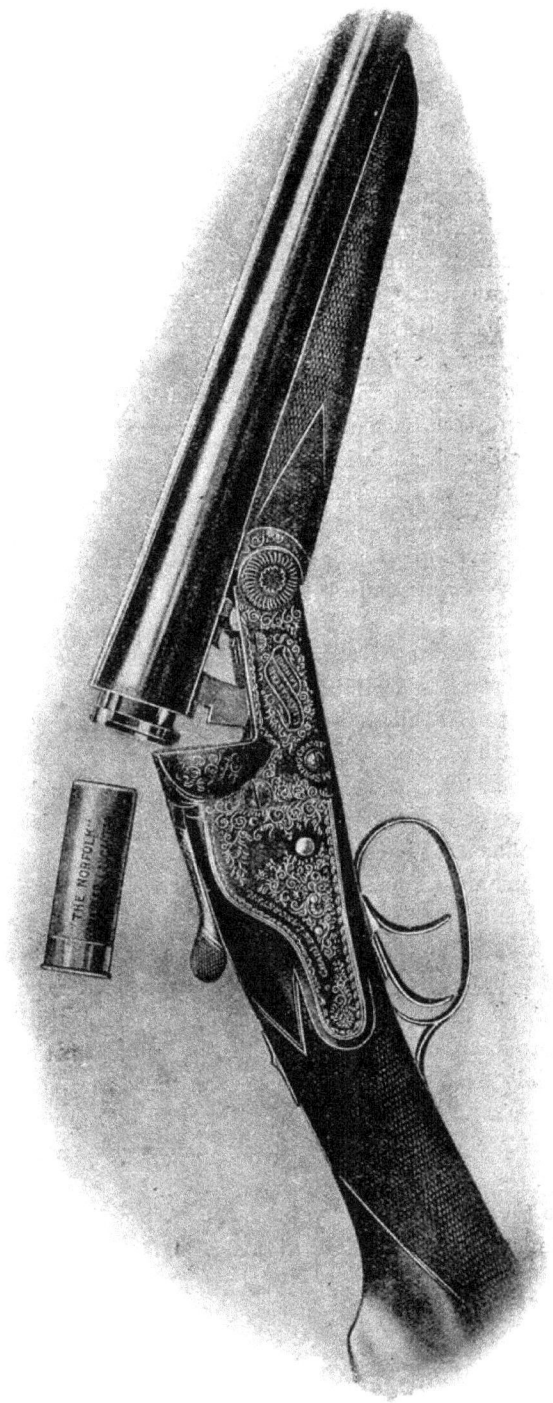

No. 66] A Side Lock Hammerless Ejector Gun, highest quality and finish, by Charles Lancaster.

If a pair of guns are required, and likely to be used very much together, then I say let all four barrels be bored to give the same pattern and penetration, and, what is of considerable importance, let all four triggers have the same pull-off, and I find 4 to 5 lbs. the best for all kinds of shooting (of course, many can, and do, have lighter pulls ; but I am speaking of shooting with a pair of guns). If choke-bores are required, then have an extra pair of barrels fitted for the purpose, although much long-distance shooting may be made with the patterns I have named—I do not mean outrageous distances, but sporting distances.

A gun to give a pattern of 140 need not be '' choke '' bored, but, as your correspondent '' Purple Heather '' styles it, a '' non-choke.''

I say by all means have your gun hammerless, but, before deciding, have the lockwork thoroughly explained to you, and see it worked (with a model, if possible) so as to be certain you are getting one in which an accidental discharge is absolutely impossible, *i.e.*, a gun that has proper blocking or intercepting bolts—a point on which the late Mr. Walsh had but one opinion. I have recommended many of my '' pupils '' to have hammerless guns, and, I believe, with every satisfaction to themselves.

The trigger safety may be automatic or independent— if for a pair of guns, where a loader's services are required, by all means *automatic*. For one gun only, automatic is to be preferred, although many have the independent action.

Certainly choose a gun that has few parts, and see that those parts are strong and simple, so that any skilled mechanic might replace one, should it become damaged in a foreign country.

Have the gun with the top lever and snap action, but see that the lever is well underset to save its damaging the thumb if by any chance it should be touching in taking a snap shot, or else the thumbnail may be hurt.

A gun that is cocked by the fall of the barrels is easier to manipulate than one that cocks with the movement of either top, side, or under lever. Always have the best barrels, whether of steel or Damascus. I have shot a great deal this season with ejectors, and, providing they are arranged so as to be on the fore-end, and independent of the lockwork, I see no reason why they should not be used.

No doubt there are ejectors and ejectors, same as there were and are hammerless and hammerless guns ; but because one fails, or requires re-regulating after a week or two's hard shooting in bad weather, it is no reason why they should not come into general use before many seasons are over, as, no doubt, they will be improved, when necessary, as time goes on.

Should an ejector be decided upon, the purchaser ought to satisfy himself that, if he should wish it to be removed, it can easily be done, and the gun then work the extraction of the cartridges in the usual manner. This should entail little or no expense afterwards.

The lighter the gun the more it will recoil, and, in some instances, "jump" unpleasantly, unless used with reduced loads. A well-balanced gun can always be handled with pleasure and quickness.

CHARLES LANCASTER.

[See page 158.]

[See footnote, page 149.]

STEEL OR DAMASCUS BARRELS.

I have read with much interest the many discussions that have taken place in the various sporting papers on this subject. I have written generally in favour of the best English Damascus barrels, which have been so long used, and have won the confidence of sportsmen, rather than advocated the use of "steel," its more modern rival.

Whitworth's Fluid Compressed Steel tubes are the best of all steel barrels; but I extract from the *Field* of the 20th October, 1888, the following opinion of Lord Walsingham, who has perhaps had a better opportunity than any living sportsman to thoroughly test the relative merits of both materials. It will prove of interest to many :—

LORD WALSINGHAM'S BAG OF GROUSE.

Many of our readers having manifested some curiosity to know the guns and charges used by Lord Walsingham on August 30th last, when, as subsequently recorded in our columns, he killed 1070 driven grouse to his own gun; his lordship, in replying to our inquiry, has been good enough to supply the following information :

" On August 30th, when I killed 1070 grouse to my own gun, in the day, I shot with four breechloaders. No. 1, a gun made in 1866 by Purdey, subsequently converted from pin-fire to central principle, to which new barrels were made last year. Nos. 2 and 3, a pair of central-fire breechloaders, made also by Purdey, about 1870, for which I have likewise had new barrels. No. 4, a new gun made by Purdey this year to match the two mentioned above, but with Whitworth steel instead of Damascus barrels. The guns are all 12-bore, with cylinder 30in. barrels, not choked. My cartridges were loaded by Johnson, of Swaffham; those used in the down-wind drives containing 3⅛drs. Hall's Field B. powder to 1⅛oz. No. 5 Derby shot; those used in the up-wind drives (where the birds, of course, came slower) had 3drs. only of the same powder, with the same shot; not hardened shot in either case.

" I find I never go out shooting without learning something. If I had the day again, I should cut off the extra eighth of an ounce of shot; not on account of recoil or discomfort of any kind—from which I never suffer, although always using black powder—but because I failed to get as much penetration at long distances as I do with an ounce only. I distinctly remember firing three barrels at one bird, striking well in the body every time, but killing dead only with the last shot; the powder seemed to burn too slow.

" Another thing I learnt was that Whitworth steel barrels are not desirable for a heavy day's shooting. The explosion in them makes quite a different sound from that given off by Damascus barrels; there is more ring about it, and I can imagine that this might prove a serious annoyance to anyone who minds the noise of shooting. I have no recollection myself of ever having had a headache from gun-firing. Moreover, the Whitworth barrels become hot much more rapidly than the Damascus; and this is a serious drawback, especially to a man who shoots without gloves. I can well imagine that they last much longer, and are in many ways suited for ordinary light work; but I am now replacing them with Damascus, as in all my other guns."

" IS MY GUN SAFE ? "

Gunmakers are frequently asked the question: " I am sending you my old guns (probably of some other maker's production) to be looked over and kept for next season, will you kindly let me know if you consider them safe, seeing that they have had several years' wear, and I am getting a little doubtful about them."

Under certain circumstances I find the following a suitable reply, viz. :—

" I cannot see that these guns have been proved for ' Nitro Powders,' this is most essential ; the best means of seeing if the guns are safe or not is, I beg to suggest, that they should be submitted to the Proof House for up-to-date proof for Nitro Powders, at owner's risk."

It is true this may be considered rather a severe strain and greater than should be borne by an old gun, but barrels are at times damaged and have required repairing from the outsides, " lapping " and polishing the insides, so are apt to lose several thousandths of their original strength, and have been proved under an earlier Gun Barrel Proof Act. I have seen barrels very badly burst at this proof—much better so, than such a thing should happen in the hands of sportsmen.

A Side Lock Single Trigger, Double Barrel, Hammerless Ejector Gun by Charles Lancaster.

No, 67]   [157

"SINGLE TRIGGER DOUBLE BARREL GUNS."

At the time of the issue of the sixth and popular edition of my treatise on " The Art of Shooting," Single Trigger Double Barrel Guns were, if I might say, quite recently re-introduced, and I received notices of my own invention by the Editor of the *Field* on June 1st, 1895, and March 21st, 1896, when full description and particulars were published. Subsequently a great deal of trouble to sportsmen, perplexing to gunmakers, had arisen, owing to the difficulty of dealing with the vagaries of Single Trigger Guns, plus a greater problem, viz., the unknown quantity of each individual shooter in the actuating of the gun whilst shooting, whereby, what has now come to be known as the " convulsive clutch " of the trigger, as the gun recedes towards the shoulder after pulling the trigger and so discharges the second barrel, has had to be dealt with and mechanically controlled in a different way; and with a view, I hope, of tersely placing this matter before sportsmen, I beg to add here the opinion of one of the " Experts," who, by the aid of the camera and the chronograph, was able to successfully diagnose what was really happening.

He says :—

" My opinion is that the second (involuntary) discharge is produced in this way. The trigger-finger presses against the trigger and discharges the first barrel. Instantly the gun leaps backward, and, owing to the elasticity of the hand (which gives way to such a sudden leap), the gun slips from the full grip and leaves, as it were, the finger behind it, releasing the trigger for the fraction of a second from the pressure of the finger. But, again, instantly the finger follows with its own convulsive energy the trigger, and with an increasing force, the result being that the second discharge takes place at about one-fiftieth of a second after the first one, but while the gun is still rapidly moving backwards, or just at the point when it begins to move with the shoulder as a solid mass. The rebound after the recoil is finally absorbed in, chronographically speaking, a very slow thing, and may be taken on the average at three-tenths of a second or more."

Charles Lancaster's Single Trigger Mechanism (Patented.)

"CHOKES" AND "CYLINDERS" OR "NON-CHOKES."

I just touch on this subject, not with the view of advocating the one or the other, but to show the difference between them. There is no doubt whatever that any gunmaker who may be consulted will be able not only to give the relative merits of each, but also to advise which is the more likely to suit the requirements of the shooter.

A "cylinder" barrel is a straight tube, of nearly the same diameter throughout, from end to end, but often relieved at muzzle and breech. The "choke" barrel is a tube, the front part of which is narrower or contracted at about half an inch from the muzzle. A mathematically true cylinder has hardly ever been sold. The "recess choke" is another form—the barrel being bored like a cylinder, and then a recess of from 2 to 4 inches is cut or spooned out from the forward portion of the barrel by the aid of a specially constructed boring tool. I have known some of my patrons who could not get on nearly so

well with a " choke " as they did with a " cylinder ; "
and having had the choke bored out, their shooting
was improved.

The penetration of both the systems, as tested at
the Pettit pads—a number (40) of sheets of stout
brown paper fastened together—is nearly equal at all
reasonable sporting distances. In the *Field* gun trial
of 1878, when six cylinders and six choke bores were
tried, 150 rounds were fired from each of the guns.
The choke bores averaged a penetration of 25 sheets
as against 23 sheets for cylinders. In each instance
the sheets had to be penetrated by three pellets.
This subject has been so often discussed, and trials
made to settle the point, that it is needless to go
further into it here ; but the above fact is generally
admitted to be correct.

Extract from the *Field*, December 25th, 1897.

"GUNS AND LOADS.

" . . . . Old Charles Lancaster, I believe, would not allow any Customer to
" talk about Patterns, much less to suggest how guns should be bored. In fact, I fancy
" he alienated many of his Patrons by the apparent shortness (I will not say brusqueness)
" of his manner. Very different is it now with the present courteous representative of the
" Old House in Bond Street.* He is always ready and willing to discuss anything and
" everything. He also was chiefly instrumental in bringing to the notice of the Public
" No. 5½ shot (medium game). It may seem to some a very significant matter, but I
" can say that 5½ shot has come out remarkably well with every 12 bore which I have
" tried with this size. . . . .

" PURPLE HEATHER."

*11, Panton Street, Haymarket.

M

CARTRIDGES.

The best cartridges should always be used, *i.e.*, those which contain the best powders and wadding, and which are carefully and accurately loaded. According to the quality of them so will be the results. By good cartridges a clean kill is obtained, and consequently more game is gathered; therefore it is a bad policy to buy cheaply and poorly loaded cartridges, to save perhaps a few shillings in the season, when by so doing the average kills are reduced, and the loss on the game is considerably greater.

The shooter who only fires a few shots a day should bear this well in mind, because he has often a long tramp between his shots, and can ill afford to find, after all his labour, that his gun is performing unevenly owing to the quality of his cartridges—or rather of their contents.

It is always an advantage to use the load recommended for the gun by its maker, and always to employ the same powder—because by the use of the same one's time is about equal, or, in other words, the velocity of the charge is not altered; consequently the judgment arrived at in aiming ahead of a bird is never beaten, and one's shooting is more regular.

"KILLS TO CARTRIDGES."

"On this question of kills to cartridges, to which I have devoted so much space, a correspondent who has been reading former volumes of the magazine writes, rather scorning the idea of the 30 per cent. which Lord Walsingham described as a fair proportion for an average good shot. Several men of his acquaintance, my correspondent declares, habitually kill at least 50 per cent., and some, he is sure, well over 50. His assertion seems to be rather based on general impressions than on careful calculation, 'I am sure,' 'I feel convinced,' 'there can really be no doubt,' being vague phrases. At easy pheasants even moderate shots may well kill a good many more than they miss, may, indeed, miss few, and if partridges lie well a man may readily make a flattering score when walking them up. Lord Walsingham's exact words were: 'Sixty in a hundred is good shooting throughout any day, but thirty is nearer the mark with most good shots if you take the season through, allowing for a fair proportion of wild game.' I have gone so fully into the matter in past numbers that I will not dilate upon it, merely adding that if anybody knows more of shooting than Lord Walsingham I should be glad to hear his name."

CHARLES LANCASTER'S "PYGMIES."

Since the earlier editions of the "Art of Shooting" were published, Powder manufacturers have turned their attention to the introduction of Powders to supersede the older "bulked up" ones, and consequently there has been in each succeeding year a very keen competition among them, and these Powders

where from 26 to 33 grains are the equivalent to 40 to 42 grains of their older patterns, have more than held their own.

These Powders admit of the introduction of shorter Cartridges, the advantage of which must be apparent to all.

The Author has had very great success with his "PYGMIES," viz., a 2″ Cartridge for 12-bore Guns only (with any length of Chamber), loaded with suitable charges of a smokeless and reliable Powder, and with one ounce or less of shot, giving high velocity, good patterns and penetration, and has hundreds of testimonials as to their " efficiency " at all sorts of game.

See the Field, May 7th, 1898.

Extract from the Field, January 8th, 1898.

SIR F. MILLBANK'S GROUSE DRIVING CHARGE.

SIR,—Apropos of guns and their loads, I believe if Sir F. Millbank was asked what charge he used when he killed 364 brace of grouse in one day, and 95 brace in one drive, he would tell you 2¾-drs. and ⅞-oz. in a 12.

" A. B. C."

[We have to thank our correspondent for his suggestion. On the above note reaching us we wrote to Sir Frederick Millbank to inquire if the facts were as stated, and, in reply, received the following very interesting letter, which we print in full.—ED.]

Dear Sir,—Your correspondent is quite right as to the charge I shot with on that memorable day's grouse shooting on Wemmergil Moor, August 20th, 1872, viz. :—

2¾-drs. Black Powder, ⅞-oz. of 6 Shot,

. . . etc., etc., etc.

FREDERICK A. MILLBANK.

Barningham Park,
  Barnard Castle.

[The above clearly demonstrates how well such a light load, especially of shot, will kill game.—ED.]

ALLOWANCE IN AIMING AT MOVING OBJECTS.

From the *Field*, March 19th, 1904.

Interesting as were the figures of striking velocities we published last week, the deductions we may now draw from them are of far greater application to the problems of every-day shooting. Unless he can see a tangible result from experimental researches, the sportsman is never quite satisfied. Hence our desire to give him an opportunity of applying the information now available to the wise selection of his ammunition and the improvement of his shooting. The ultimate test of abstract research is that it shall be capable of application, and in the present instance we can fully satisfy this somewhat difficult requirement. On the basis of the figures which were published last week we can inform the sportsman the exact allowance he must give to a crossing bird according to the range at which the shot is taken.

To analyse the values of striking velocity at every distance, as published in our last issue, we first of all converted them into the following table of mean velocities between the muzzle of the gun and the various distances into which the range was divided :—

Size of shot.	Distance over which the mean velocities are specified.				
	0—20 yds.	0—25 yds.	0—30 yds.	0—35 yds.	0—40 yds.
3	1050	1009	971	944	903
4	1050	1005	962	929	888
5	1050	1003	959	923	882
5½	1050	1001	955	917	876
6	1050	1000	952	912	871
6½	1050	998	949	906	865
7	1050	996	946	901	860

All velocities are stated in feet per second.

From this table we gather that a charge of No. 6 shot fired from a standard cartridge having a velocity of 1,050 ft. per

second over 20 yards has a mean velocity of 952 ft. over
30 yards, and 871 ft. over 40 yards. The corresponding values
for the other sizes of shot are similarly set forth in the above
table, and we see from it that there is a difference in the mean
velocity over 40 yards of 43 ft. between shot sizes 3 and 7.
This means that, although the 20 yards' mean velocity is
equal in all cases, the greater ranging power of the larger sizes
of shot gives them a distinct advantage in mean velocity at
all sporting ranges beyond that of 20 yards, which infers that
the large sizes of shot reach the bird quicker than the smaller
sizes, and, in the absence of definite quantities, it would appear
as though a distinctly greater allowance must be given, say,
in the case of No. 7 shot as compared with No. 4. Having a
really authoritative set of relations to work upon, it is obviously
the best plan to reduce these differences to actual quantities
in inches of allowance.

The time occupied between the fall of the hammer and the
arrival of the shot at a given distance is naturally not included
in the time value derived from the mean velocity from the
muzzle to the object struck, and we must accordingly add
the amount of time occupied from the fall of the hammer to
the arrival of the charge of shot at the muzzle. Persons of
an over-refining turn of mind might be inclined to argue that
an extra time allowance should be made in respect to the
interval between the brain signal that the gun is properly
aligned and the response of the finger by way of pulling the
trigger. This may, however, be dismissed, for the reason
that, if the swing of the gun is continuously maintained, the
processes of the shooter's mind may for all practical purposes
be ignored. In this way the distance of the bird's flight
while the shot is reaching it must date, so to speak, from the
fall of the hammer to the impact of the shot.

We have accordingly reduced the mean velocities shown
in the first table to a series of time values, which are

represented in the form of decimal fractions of a second. To each of the values so obtained we added an allowance of ·0040 of a second for the delay in the gun above referred to. The following table of values accordingly represents the time which elapses with each size of shot from the fall of the hammer to the arrival of the charge at the various distances named :—

Size of shot.	Points on range for which time delays are specified.				
	20 yds.	25 yds.	30 yds.	35 yds.	40 yds.
3	·0611	·0783	·0967	·1162	·1369
4	·0611	·0786	·0975	·1177	·1391
5	·0611	·0788	·0979	·1184	·1401
5½	·0611	·0789	·0982	·1189	·1411
6	·0611	·0790	·0985	·1194	·1418
6¼	·0611	·0792	·0988	·1200	·1427
7	·0611	·0793	·0991	·1205	·1435

All times are stated in decimals of a second.

As figures are never very interesting unless the mind can grasp their actual meaning, our comments upon this table shall be very brief. All we wish to point out is that when the differences in the times of arrival are represented to the nearest ten-thousandth part of a second they appear quite considerable. For instance, at 40 yards there is a time interval of ·0066 of a second between the arrival of a charge of No. 3 shot and a charge of No. 7 shot. The question to be settled is how far the bird will travel during this interval of time, the value shown by such a calculation being the amount of extra allowance that must be accorded to No. 7 shot as compared with No. 3.

Now, in order to produce a table of allowances, for aiming at moving objects, it is necessary to adopt a characteristic rate of flight as a basis for comparison. We accordingly adopted the value of 60 ft. per second, which corresponds with forty miles an hour, and is the average rate of flight which we have ourselves fixed by chronograph measurements for a clay bird sprung from a powerful trap and throwing at an angle with the ground more or less horizontal. It is similarly the recognised speed of a fast-flying pheasant or a driven grouse or partridge. Almost needless to say, many birds fly much slower than this, whereas others move along at a greater rate when the wind is in their favour and when the rate of flight is aided by gravity, as is the case when a bird is flushed on a hill and is inclining its course towards a lower elevation. To obtain the distance covered in a given time by a bird travelling at 60 ft. per second is a very simple matter. The values in the above table of time allowances must be multiplied by sixty, the number of feet covered in a second. The result is the number of feet the bird will cover in the fraction of time used in the sum. Without further preface, we will introduce our third table, which shows the exact distance a bird will travel during the time that elapses from the fall of the hammer to the arrival of the various sizes of shot at the distances named :—

TABLE OF ALLOWANCES FOR AIMING AT A CROSSING BIRD.

Size of shot.	Distance of bird when the hammer falls.				
	20 yds.	25 yds.	30 yds.	35 yds.	40 yds.
3	3ft. 8·0in.	4ft. 7·4in.	5ft. 9·6in.	6ft. 11·7in.	8ft. 2·6in.
4	3 ,, 8·0 ,,	4 ,, 8·6 ,,	5 ,, 10·2 ,,	7 ,, 0·7 ,,	8 ,, 4·1 ,,
5	3 ,, 8·0 ,,	4 ,, 8·7 ,,	5 ,, 10·5 ,,	7 ,, 1·2 ,,	8 ,, 4·9 ,,
5½	3 ,, 8·0 ,,	4 ,, 8·8 ,,	5 ,, 10·7 ,,	7 ,, 1·6 ,,	8 ,, 5·6 ,,
6	3 ,, 8·0 ,,	4 ,, 8·9 ,,	5 ,, 10·9 ,,	7 ,, 2·0 ,,	8 ,, 6·1 ,,
6½	3 ,, 8·0 ,,	4 ,, 9·0 ,,	5 ,, 11·1 ,,	7 ,, 2·4 ,,	8 ,, 6·7 ,,
7	3 ,, 8·0 ,,	4 ,, 9·1 ,,	5 ,, 11·4 ,,	7 ,, 2·8 ,,	8 ,, 7·3 ,,

Here we have in an absolutely tangible form an important portion of the lesson that is to be learnt from the series of investigations which culminated in the table published in our last issue. We find that in shooting at 20 yards the same allowance is required for all sizes of shot, the amount being 3 ft. 8 in., which is thus far greater than many would suppose. At 25 yards the required allowance is increased by practically another foot. At 30 yards there is a rather greater proportional increase, while at 35 yards the allowance becomes the very substantial one of 7 ft. or more. At 40 yards the shooter who desires to centre his charge of shot on a fast-flying bird travelling at right angles to the line of flight must aim rather more than 8 ft. in front of it.

Turning now to the differences in the specified allowances for the extreme sizes of shot shown in the table, it will be seen that up to 30 yards they are less than 2 in. At 35 yards the separation of values becomes more pronounced, and the difference is, practically speaking, 3 in., while at 40 yards it attains a maximum of just under 5 in. These figures entirely disprove the assumption that the shooter requires to alter his allowance when aiming at moving objects according to the size of shot in his gun. Adopting No. 6 shot as a standard size, we find that there is a difference of only 2 in. in the allowance for a 40-yards shot when a change is made to size No. 4. In view of the impossibility of knowing the precise velocity of the cartridge, the true range of the bird, and its correct rate of flight, it is obvious that such fractional differences as are created by a change in the size of shot are too infinitesimal for serious consideration. We accordingly adopt the allowance shown for size No. 6, and draw up the following exceedingly simple code of instructions to the shooter who desires to have a tangible idea of the allowance that he must give to a fast-flying bird :—

When the bird is at 20 yards the shooter must allow 3 ft. 8 in.
,,   ,,   25 ,,   ,,   ,,   4 ft. 9 in.
,,   ,,   30 ,,   ,,   ,,   5 ft. 11 in.
,,   ,,   35 ,,   ,,   ,,   7 ft. 2 in.
,,   ,,   40 ,,   ,,   ,,   8 ft. 6 in.

As already stated, the above allowances only represent the daylight between the bird and the point at which aim should be taken in the case of crossing shots. When a bird's flight is inclined so as to produce a foreshortening effect of its line of travel, the distance it covers is still the same, but the amount of daylight between the bird and the point at which aim is taken is a reducing quantity, which culminates at the zero mark when the bird is flying either directly towards or directly away from the shooter. This question of angle is, however, one which the shooter must instinctively settle for himself. If he knows approximately that the bird will move, say, 7 ft. while the shot is reaching it, he must decide in his own mind, according to the angle at which the bird is flying, whether this must represent 1 ft., 2 ft., or 3 ft., as the case may be, of daylight between the bird and the point aimed at.

There is, however, another aspect of the question, which raises an apparent difficulty in the application of the above figures. Supposing that the bird is directly going away, and that its distance is 35 yards at the moment when the hammer falls, the bird will naturally have moved 7 ft. 2 in., not by the time that it is struck, but by the time the shot has reached the distance of the bird when the hammer fell. During the time that the shot is covering the 35 yards already mentioned the bird still continues its flight. Consequently, some further time must elapse while the shot is covering the extra 7 ft. 2 in. Referring to our curve of values we find that the average velocity of a No. 6 pellet between 35 and 38 yards may be taken at 680 ft. per second. Under such circumstances, the bird will move a further 7·67 in. while the shot is travelling the extra 7 ft. 2 in. It thus happens that the total flight of a going-away bird at 30 yards between the fall of the hammer and the impact of the shot on the feathers is as nearly as possible 7 ft. 10 in., instead of the 7 ft. 2 in. for a crossing bird. As, however, no allowance is necessary in the case of an approaching or going-away bird, this difference is absolutely immaterial, except in so far that the shot does not strike the bird with the velocity it possesses when at the 35 yards mark.

Referring again to our curve, we find that the striking velocity of the shot at the moment when it reaches a bird at 35 yards is 695 ft. per second. This velocity is reduced to 670 ft. per second when the bird has travelled a further 7 ft. 9 in., and if we deduct 60 ft. from the striking velocity by reason of the fact that the shot is not colliding with a stationary object, but one moving away at about one-tenth of its own velocity, then we find that the actual velocity of impact of a going-away bird shot at when 25 yards away, becomes 610 ft. per second. This enables us to lay down that the velocity with which the shot strikes a going-away bird, shot at when 35 yards distant, is the same as that of shooting at a crossing bird 44 yards away.

From the point of view of the actual flight of the bird during the travel of the shot it will be found that the perspective foreshortening of the line of flight for semi-crossing birds makes it entirely unnecessary to increase the allowance by reason of the fact that the bird is increasing its distance from the shooter while the shot is travelling up the range. The resolving of our calculations into the very simple series of figures which are given above may thus be considered all sufficient for practical purposes. We have laid down the necessary allowances that must be made in the case of cartridges having a standard velocity. In the future we shall be able to examine cartridges which depart from this standard, either by showing an excess or a decrease on the standard velocity laid down, and we shall be able to show in inches the differences of allowance which arise from abnormal cartridges, whether they be on the strong or on the weak side. A careful examination of our tabulated results enables us to say that we shall be able to ascertain the striking velocity at all distances of any cartridge by making the very simple time measurement involved in ascertaining the mean velocity between 15 and 25 yards. We have shown that from the muzzle to 20 yards' velocity test affords a splendid insight into the general characteristics of a cartridge. We shall, in the future, be able to show that its effectiveness from the sportsman's standpoint may best be tested between 15 and 25 yards. It would be unfair to anticipate the teachings of experiments yet to be made. We can, therefore, dismiss the subject for the moment, now that we have stated the exact allowances that must be made at all sporting distances for cartridges giving a standard velocity.

STRIKING VELOCITIES OF SHOT, AT ALL RANGES.

From the *Field*, March 26th, 1904.

Following up last week's record of experiments to determine the striking velocities of different shot sizes, we are now in a position to put forward the logical conclusion of our work. It will be remembered that in the previous article we showed how the flight of Nos. 3 and 7 shot had been traced from the muzzle to 30 yards up the range, and we further gave our reasons for the belief that the remainder of the flight of the shot should be expressed by means of calculations based on Bashforth's formulæ. It was also pointed out that the behaviour of the intermediate sizes of shot could be estimated with the greatest exactitude by reason of our knowledge of the behaviour of the extreme sizes.

We here reproduce a table giving certain particulars concerning the various sizes of shot dealt with, which will doubtless be of interest for reference purposes to those who are inclined to make a close study of the subject :—

Size of pellet.	Pellets per oz.	Weight per pellet.	Relative blow at equal velocity.	Diameter of pellet.	Sectional area.	Value of $\dfrac{W}{d^2}$	Relative penetrative power.
		grs.		in.	sq. in.		
3	140	3·13	193	·127	·0127	194·1	124·67
4	172	2·54	157	·120	·0113	176·2	113·17
5	218	2·01	124	·109	·0093	169·1	108·61
5½	240	1·82	112	·106	·0088	162·0	104·05
6	**270**	**1·62**	**100**	**·102**	**·0082**	**155·7**	**100**
6½	300	1·46	90	·099	·0077	149·0	95·70
7	340	1·29	80	·095	·0071	142·9	91·78

At any rate, the tabulated particulars therein given have formed the groundwork of calculations for determining the theoretical values used for checking our experimental observations. The first column relates to the size of the pellet, the second to the number contained in the ounce, and the third shows the weight of each pellet to the nearest hundredth of a grain. The fourth column is very interesting, in so far that it gives the relative striking energy of each size of pellet under conditions of equal velocity. We have treated No. 6 shot as having a striking energy proportional to 100, the other sizes of shot being shown in true proportion to this value. The figures given are, as a matter of fact, merely the proportional weights of the different sizes dealt with, but even so their relation in this respect is clearer when stated on the basis of a round number for the standard size of No. 6. The figures contained in the column showing the diameter of the pellets have already been published. It is, however, necessary to repeat them, because the values are different from those that have been adopted by earlier experimentalists. They were obtained by placing 100 pellets of each size of shot in the crease formed by the folding of a piece of paper. The mean diameter per pellet was obtained by dividing the length of the string of 100 pellets by their total number. This gave a very exact figure for the diameter, care, of course, having been taken to ensure the conformity of the samples examined with the nominal count of pellets per ounce. The sectional area of the pellets is useful, as showing the surface which is exposed to the resistance of the air. The adjoining column, which gives the mathematical ratio obtained by dividing the weight in grains by the square of the diameter, shows the relative driving power of different sizes of shot through the air, and equally their penetrative power into solid objects. For

convenience of comparison these same values are expressed in
the last column of the table so multiplied out that the penetrative power of No. 6 shot is expressed as 100, the others being
in true relation with this value.

A pellet of No. 3 shot has a striking velocity of 706 ft. per
second at 40 yards, that of a No. 7 pellet being 629 ft. per
second. These are the striking velocities of two pellets of
shot whose relative ranging power is represented in the last
column of the above table by the figures 124·67 and 91·78
respectively. The net difference of striking velocity which
exists between these two pellets at 40 yards range is 77 ft.
To build up a complete table of striking velocities it was
necessary to allocate this interval of 77 ft. in suitable proportion
among the intermediate sizes of shot. A little calculation
showed that 12 per cent. of this 77 ft. should be added to the
velocity of No. 7 shot to obtain the value for size No. 6½.
No. 6 shot required an addition equal to 25 per cent. of
the 77 ft., No. 5½, 37 per cent., No. 5, 51 per cent., and
No. 4, 66 per cent. In this way it became clear that by
adding 9, 19, 28, 39, and 51 ft. to the striking velocity at
40 yards of No. 7 shot, we should obtain the closest possible
estimate of the striking velocities of the sizes of shot lying
between the extremes of 7 and 3. At 35 yards there was a
difference of 70 ft. between the extremes, at 30 yards 62 ft.,
and so forth. Each of these differences between Nos. 3 and 7
shot was carefully divided in the above proportions, and the
appropriate values of velocity for each range were thus allocated
to the intermediate sizes of shot.

A complete table of striking velocities was thus built up,
and the values obtained were subjected to a very careful
arithmetical analysis, slight corrections being made to ensure
a true descent of the curve. The final figures are here given,

and it will be noticed that we have included a full range of values for 5¼ shot, although a curve for the same does not appear in the diagram :—

TABLE OF SHOT VELOCITY at various ranges from 10 to 40 yards, for standard cartridges giving 1,050 ft. per second over 20 yards, this being the absolute velocity at about 9 yards.

Size of shot.	Distance from Muzzle in yards.						
	10	15	20	25	30	35	40
3	1038	960	896	841	791	746	706
4	1036	953	884	824	771	723	680
5	1036	949	876	814	759	711	668
5½	1035	946	871	807	751	701	657
6	1034	944	868	803	746	695	649
6½	1034	941	862	794	735	683	638
7	1033	938	858	789	729	676	629

All velocities are given in feet per second.

It is very interesting to compare the relative striking velocities at the different distances, though, of course, the effects are best seen in the last column, which relates to the 40 yards distance. Between 6 and 7 shot there is a difference of 20 ft., which seems fully to justify the recognition which we have claimed for the 6½ size, which occupies a very appropriate middle position. Between 6 and 5 shot there is a separation of 19 ft., which seems again to afford a thorough justification for size 5½. Between sizes 4 and 5 there is a difference of only 12 ft. in the velocity, this seeming to show the irregularity of the intervals that separate the whole sizes of shot. There is a gap of 26 ft. between sizes 3 and 4, though one would naturally expect this difference to increase as we reach the higher sizes. It is none the less clear, however, that from sizes 5 to 7 the existence of intermediate half divisions is an absolute necessity in order that shooters should be able to adjust the patterns given by their guns to the

N

required nicety. A large amount of speculative analysis could be based on the relative velocities of the different sizes of shot at different ranges; but there is not space at the present time to enter at all in detail into this very interesting question. It is sufficient for the moment to know that for the first time in English gunnery we have before us a really well authenticated series of striking velocities at various distances for all the sizes of shot which are commonly in use among sportsmen. While the differences of velocity shown are by no means as great as some might expect, it must be remembered that the striking energy of shot pellets is in proportion to the square of their velocity. Hence the energy difference is much greater than that of the simple velocity. When, again, we remember that the energy is directly proportional to the weight of the pellet, it will be evident that this represents another source of separation between the values given. The first table reproduced in this article shows that at equal velocities a No. 7 pellet has only 80 per cent. of the striking power of one No. 6 size. Another complication arises from the fact that as shot pellets become smaller so the number striking an object is apt to increase. Hence the need for a third qualification in the direct application of the figures which are here published.

THE PHYSIOLOGY OF SHOOTING.

BY WM. JAS. FLEMING, M.D.

From the *Field* of February 19th, 1887.

It is universally admitted that good shooting depends less upon the gun than upon the man behind it. The gun and all connected with it have received, and still receive, most minute and careful study, but little attention has been devoted to the human element in marksmanship. In so far as shooting goes, the man is as purely a machine as the gun, but a much more complicated and less understood piece of mechanism, and, to make the problem worse, an individual mechanism—no two quite alike. There are, however, some principles and arrangements common to every human shooting machine which can be formulated, and in this paper I will try to place them as clearly as possible before my readers. For this purpose it will only be necessary to consider the problems connected with shooting at moving objects, as this embraces all the questions arising out of target practice.

To begin with, let us try to analyse the processes which result in a bird coming down a few yards from where it rose near a good shot. First, he sees the bird—that is to say, the image of the bird is sharply focussed on his retina by the proper adjustment of the internal mechanism of the eye. In this retina the picture thrown upon it sets up nervous changes, which are conveyed to some part of the brain, and there produce what we call vision—in reality, a change in some part of the nervous tissue of the brain. At the same time he judges the distance of the bird and the direction and rate of its flight by a complicated process, of which more hereafter. The information thus gained is transformed at first by an effort of will, but, after sufficient practice, automatically, into orders affecting nearly all the muscles of the body. He plants his feet firmly and raises his gun (for simplicity sake here we will suppose he is a shot who takes aim—a question afterwards to be discussed). Having raised the gun, he looks along it, and, I believe, by a continual alteration of the focus of his eye, sees both the sight and the bird at one time, and waits till they are in one line. Again this state of affairs is communicated to the brain by the eye, and an order sent to the finger to pull the trigger ; then the mechanism is all gun. It is all done in the fraction of a second, but it must all be done, and really much more.

I must now endeavour to explain the above somewhat more fully, but will take it for granted that the reader knows enough of ordinary optics to require no more detailed explanation of how the bird is seen, only remarking that it is by no means an instantaneous process.

Seeing the bird, how does he judge its distance from him ? *By the summation of the various adjustments his eyes require to make to see clearly, compared with previous experience.* The principal of these adjustments are the amount of convergence of the two eyes required to bring their optical axes to a point at the bird, and the amount of accommodation necessary to bring the image of the bird to a sharp focus on the retina.

These adjustments are made by muscles both without and within the eye, and we are informed of their amount by the *muscular sense*. This muscular sense is really the keynote of the whole question, and therefore requires some further explanation.

It is not generally known that we possess a distinct power of appreciating the amount of muscular force required to perform an action, quite separate from our sense of touch. Perhaps the best way to understand this is to consider the different effects of, say, a pound weight laid upon our palm with the back of the hand resting upon the table, and the same weight lifted freely up and down, as we instinctively do in estimating weight. In the first case we feel the pressure of a cold, hard body, but, if not aided by sight, have a very faint idea of its weight ; indeed, we can scarcely tell the difference between one and two pounds if the surfaces touching the palm are of nearly the same area, and if the objects are gently deposited, the eyes being shut, and the hand motionless and supported. If, however, the weights are lifted by the arm, we at once appreciate the difference. This muscular sense plays a very important part in our lives, and is peculiarly capable of training. A good example of this is the power acquired by letter-sorters in the post office to detect by the hand alone the slightest over-weight, a practised hand rarely erring. It is by this muscular sense, telling us how much we have required to use the muscles both within and without the eye, that we estimate distance.

To return to the bird, we have seen that a series of complicated processes are necessary merely to see it and judge approximately its distance ; but, aided by experience, we learn by means of the same mechanism, and practically simultaneously, a great deal more about it—the angle in relation to our position at which it is flying, an idea of the pace it is going, &c. Having unconsciously, or at least, apparently so, got all this information, which, of course, is largely due to practice, the brain condition thus set up induces (in what physiologists call an automatic manner) a large number of muscular actions—planting the feet, raising the gun, and in the case of the man who aims, which we are now considering, closing one eye and bringing the other to a place in relation to the gun suitable for aligning the barrel with the bird ; then information is carried to the brain that the gun is " on," and an order sent to the finger to pull the trigger. In the case of the man who shoots with both eyes open and the head erect—who, in fact, does not look along the gun at all—we have a somewhat different order of proceeding. He estimates in the same way the distance, direction, and rapidity of flight ; but having done this, trusts entirely to his muscular sense to hold the gun straight and to tell him when it is straight. To succeed in this can only be the result of practice ; but we must remember that the muscular sense varies enormously in accuracy and rapidity of expression in different men, and even in the same man at different times and under different conditions. Some men hear, see, taste, smell better than others ; why should we wonder that they differ in this sense also, or that one individual requires more training or practice than another to achieve the same accuracy ?

This difference between individuals is not confined to their muscular sense, but exists in an even more marked way in the amount of time required by each to go through the complicated nervous and muscular actions which I have described. Atten-tion was first drawn to this by the astronomers, who found that it is necessary to allow for what is called " personal error," in the observations of different individuals. For instance, suppose it is required to observe the exact moment at which a star touches a hair stretched across the field of a stationary telescope, and that by a suitable arrangement two observers are enabled to watch through the telescope at the same time—it will be found that an appreciable difference exists in the record of each. What is more, this difference will be practically constant for the same individual, constituting his " personal equation," which has to be allowed for in subsequent calculations. By modifications of this idea, physiologists have succeeded in measuring, not only the time taken by the whole process, but the time occupied by each of its component parts.

To go into the details of these experiments is needless here, but, in order to give a general idea of the methods employed, it may be well to describe one or two of them. Let us take first the one which has been perhaps best worked out—the determination of the rapidity with which an impulse travels along a nerve. If we arrange a stimulus—most conveniently an electric shock—so that when applied, let us suppose over a nerve in the forearm, it causes a contraction of the muscles of a finger, and consequently a movement of the finger, and if we measure the exact time which elapses between the electric shock and the movement of the finger, first when the stimulus is applied, say, nine inches from the finger, and again three inches from the finger, the difference will give us the time taken for transmission through the six inches, and therefore the rate.

Some of the readers of this article may be interested in the apparatus employed in making these delicate measurements, so I will briefly describe the essential features. We require a surface moving rapidly and regularly, upon which a faint motion can easily make a mark. This is generally obtained by a large cylinder rotated by clockwork, and covered with smoked paper. Upon this are inscribed, by light contact, motions, however slight, communicated to

levers. For the experiment just mentioned, to determine
the rapidity of transmission of nervous impulses, three of
these levers would be required—one attached to the finger
to be moved, one actuated by the same electric current which
gives the shock, and one connected with a chronograph or
instrument for marking time. This is generally a tuning
fork, the number of whose vibrations is known, and of course
constant. If, then, with the three levers adjusted to write
exactly perpendicular to each other, the cylinder is rotated,
we shall have three straight lines drawn. If, now, the tuning
fork is made to vibrate, the lever attached to it will mark
curves, and if, now, the electric shock is sent into the nerve,
the lever connected with it will move and mark the exact
moment of stimulation. As soon as the muscles of the finger
begin to respond to the stimulus, the lever attached to the
finger will mark, and the difference between the two, read
by the vibrations of the tuning fork, which have been going
on all the time, gives the time of transmission. Our tracing
then will be something like this, and the distance between
the lines a and a, read on the tuning fork the actual time of

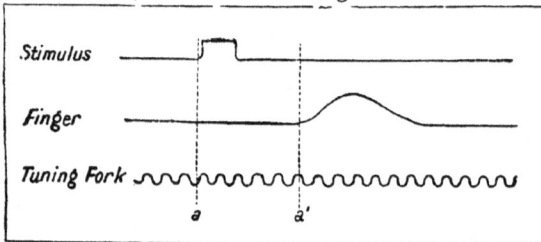

nervous transmission, less the latent period of the muscle,
which we need not consider in this case. By this experiment,
more or less modified, it has been calculated that the rate
of transmission of motor stimuli in man is only 120 feet per
second. Your readers will remember that shot at 40 yards
travels at the rate of about 600 feet per second.

To estimate the time taken by the whole process, for the conversion of a visual image into a voluntary muscular action —which is exactly what takes place between seeing a bird and pulling the trigger—a slightly different arrangement is required. The person to be experimented upon is seated with his finger on an electrical key, so arranged that the moment it is depressed, a mark is recorded upon the revolving cylinder. A blue and red light are fixed so that either can be shown at the option of the experimenter. The subject of the experiment is directed only to depress the key when one of those lights is shown, and the instant at which this light is exposed is also recorded upon the cylinder. A chronograph is used as before. By this means we are able to estimate the whole time taken by both the nervous transmission and the mental judgment of which of the two lights was shown. The result of a number of experiments on these lines give for different individuals from $\frac{1}{100}$ of a second to $\frac{6}{100}$ of a second. Now, if we consider that this corresponds to the interval between the gunner seeing the bird and pulling the trigger, we can easily calculate that if the bird is crossing at the rate of 50 feet per second—practically thirty-four miles an hour —in the case of a man with $\frac{1}{100}$ of a second personal error, it will only have flown 6 inches, whereas, in the case of the man with $\frac{6}{100}$ it will have flown 3 feet. This seems largely to explain why men differ so much in the amount they borrow. The lesson is that each individual must find out the proper " borrow " for himself, as another person, with probably quite a different personal error, cannot guide him.

A great deal has been written lately in your columns on the two methods of borrowing, which I may summarise as " swing " and " carry forward." Upon this also the above considerations may throw some light. By " swing " I understand keeping the gun moving with the object for a short time before firing. Your correspondents are not at one about this, it appears to me, because they do not consider what is taking place during the time between the determination to pull and the explosion of the powder. If during this interval the swing is arrested (as I fancy it often is), then the gun must be pointed considerably in front of the object; but if it is kept up, that is to say, if the gun is kept pointed at the object until the shot has left the barrel, a very small allowance is necessary—merely the time taken by the shot to reach the object. Indeed, the swing of the gun must to some extent do away even with this, in the same way that a heavy object thrown from a rapidly moving train does not fly at a right angle to the train, but has the train's forward motion communicated to it as well as the motion of throwing, and therefore assumes the direction of the resultant of these two forces—outwards and forwards.

In what I have described as the carry-forward method of borrowing (which I conceive is less often actually employed than is supposed), the idea is to fire into the air where the bird will be when the shot reaches that place. Now, this may do for the man of very slight personal error, but for the man of great personal error seems to me impracticable, from the immense distance it would entail firing in front. A good many who think they practise this method probably swing the gun into a position in front of the object, stop the swing, and fire. By this it is obvious that they only need to allow for the time between deciding to fire and the shot reaching the place; but a man who fires where the bird will be without any swing, must allow for all the time of deciding how far forward to shoot, raising his gun to that, and then the time of firing and travel of shot.

I am sorry I cannot suggest any simple means by which sportsmen could ascertain the amount of their personal error, as the apparatus I have described is not easily attainable ; but perhaps some of our enterprising gun-makers might find it pay them to have such an apparatus for the benefit of their customers. I shall be glad to advise as to such an installation. I have long been of opinion that very good shots are generally men with small personal error, and such an arrangement would enable the truth of this idea to be investigated.

Another important point in connection with this matter is the influence, noticed by all observers, which food, stimulants, and sedative, have in altering the figures for each individual. The effects vary in different persons, and this goes far to account for some men shooting better before, others after, lunch, for some men being unable to shoot if they smoke, others unable to shoot if they do not. I have tried to show that each must be a law to himself, and therefore, I trust, helped some men who have failed to get good results by following the rules of their mentors.

From "THE FIELD," *July 9th, 1898.*

By Special Permission.

THE NATURALIST.

SPEED OF BIRDS.

A VERY interesting example of the rate of flight in birds has recently occurred. The performance is an exceptional one, and is the best that has taken place in this country. Mr. Clutterbuck, of Stanmore, a very enthusiastic homing pigeon flier, who has spared neither expense nor trouble in obtaining and training the best birds, on Monday, June 27th, won the race from the Shetland Islands. The distance flown was 591½ miles, and was accomplished eight minutes under sixteen hours. The birds were liberated at Lerwick, Shetland Islands, at 3.30 a.m., the wind and weather being favourable. The rate may be taken at thirty-seven miles per hour. Had not the birds been liberated at such an early hour in the morning, they could not have reached home that day, inasmuch as they rarely, if ever, fly after 8 p.m. In estimating the speed of this flight of homing pigeons it must be taken into consideration that the wind was favourable during the whole course. It will be seen by the copy of the weather chart of the Meteorological Office for the day, that after leaving the Shetland Islands, where the wind was north-west, in the rest of the course the wind was due north, and this continued the whole day, the chart being made up for 6 p.m., favouring in every mile of the journey the flight of the birds, and the

CHART SHOWING DIRECTION OF WIND.

breezes were during the whole day strong to fresh ; so that no conditions could possibly have been more advantageous to the rapid flight from north to south.

As I do not know of any long-distance flight in which the conditions as regards time and the direction and force of the wind have been so accurately noted, I regard this performance as one that should be permanently recorded as important to ornithologists.

It is satisfactory to me to note that the utilisation of homing pigeons for marine and other Government services, which I advocated in the *Times* more than a quarter of a century since, has at last come to pass, and in a recent issue of that journal I find that the Odessa correspondent writes as follows :—

The new Russian pigeon club, which is under Government superintendence, and whose members are mostly officers, is giving many prizes this summer for pigeon-flying between Odessa and Constantinople, Odessa and Sulina, Odessa and Varna, and Sevastopol and Constantinople. The pastime is intended to be of practical value whenever use may be found by the Government for its services,

The utilisation of pigeons for military service has long been followed on the Continent.   W. B. TEGETMEIER.

SPEED IN THE FLIGHT OF BIRDS.

Extract from a Norfolk Paper, March 16th, 1901.

If you consult the usually accepted authorities on the speed of birds in their flight, says the *New York Herald*, you are likely to be misled by an exaggeration of from 100 to 300 per cent. This is because figures have been given on hearsay, appearances, and very superficial observation. But recently American, English, and French observers have been comparing notes, and are practically agreed, after most careful calculation, on the speed of the best known birds. They started with the carrier pigeon, and have made him a base of comparison. He has heretofore been credited with one hundred and ten miles an hour, but it is now agreed that he is entitled to fifty. A quite recent long distance, carefully conducted test, of five hundred and ninety-two miles, from the Shetland Isles to London, showed that the most rapid pigeons made thirty-seven miles an hour. On shorter distances none made more than fifty miles.

Because frigate birds have been seen far from land, and have been supposed not to fly by night or to rest on the water, they have been credited with a speed of from one hundred and fifty to two hundred miles an hour. If they did fly at that speed they would have to overcome an atmospheric pressure of from one hundred and twelve to one hundred and thirty pounds to the square foot of flying surface. There is no certainty that they fly more rapidly than a passenger pigeon, or that they do not fly at night or do not sleep on the water.

The swallow, that is indeed a rapid flier, has been credited with a hundred and eighty miles an hour, but he must be cut down to sixty-five miles, and the marten is five miles behind him, though authorities have placed him ten ahead.

The teal duck is brought down from a hundred and forty to fifty miles an hour. The mallard is five miles slower, and flies the same as the canvasback, while both of these are five miles an hour ahead of the wild goose and eider duck.

The pheasant makes thirty-eight miles an hour, which is three miles ahead of the prairie chicken and quail, though the latter appears to fly much faster on account of his temporary bursts of speed, that seldom exceed two hundred feet. The crow flies twenty-five miles an hour.

Small birds appear to fly more rapidly than the large ones, and have deceived many observers. The humming bird does not fly as fast as many awkward appearing, very much larger, slow flapping birds.

The most satisfactory tests of speed have been made on extended tracts of level land, where timekeepers with stop watches stand on lines at given distances apart, and time the shadows of the flying birds as they pass from one line to another.

VELOCITY OF THE FLIGHT OF BIRDS.

Very different opinions are often expressed as to the speed of game birds when in full flight; and no doubt much of the difference of opinion is due to the variations that arise from the amount of assistance derived from the wind. Some persons think that pigeons are faster than the generality of game birds, and others the reverse. There is much more information available with respect to pigeons than with regard to game birds, owing to the number of races which continually occur with homing pigeons; and the following letter from Mr. Tegetmeier, which appeared in the *Field* of January 22, 1887, gives some detailed information on the subject. It will be seen that in some of the races the speed of the birds was more than double what it was in others; but it must be remembered that pigeons make their way homewards, whether the winds be favourable or adverse; and consequently, in some of these instances the birds were greatly assisted by the wind, while in others they were retarded.

The question as to the rate at which birds fly is one which has recently attracted considerable attention, and very erroneous guesses have been hazarded. There is only one bird of which we have any authentic and reliable record of its rate of flight, namely, the homing pigeon.

In the races which take place in this country and on the Continent, the exact time at which the birds are liberated is recorded, and the moment they reach their homes the number (previously unknown to the owner), which has been stamped on the flight feathers, is telegraphed by him to the secretary of the race, hence the returns are most reliable.

The velocities attained in the different races vary very greatly with the state of the weather, for, as the birds fly by sight, they are much hindered by mist or a dull atmosphere, and they are also greatly affected by the force and direction of the wind. The only fair mode of proceeding, therefore, is to take the average of a number of races, which would necessarily include those flown under divers conditions as to atmospheric influences.

The following table gives the result of the races flown by the United Counties Flying Club in the year 1883 ; the velocity in yards per minute of the fastest bird in each race is given, and in the following column the number of miles flown, and also the points of departure and arrival :

No.	Velocity in Yards per minute.	Miles Flown.
1	1240	136—Swindon to Lowton.
2	963	195—Salisbury to Barrowford.
3	1620	208—Ventnor to Manchester.
4	992	270—Cherbourg to Manchester.
5	443	121—Ventnor to Worcester.
6	732	201—Cherbourg to East Langton.
7	935	269—Granville to Lullington.
8	1145	309—Rennes to Church Langton.
9	898	144—Cherbourg to Cardiff.
10	990	175—Granville to Devizes.
11	1271	224—Rennes to Devizes.
12	804	129—Cherbourg to Reading.
13	916	168—Granville to Bexhill.
14	1406	232—Rennes to Sunningdale.
15	1293	87—Worcester to Audenshaw.
16	1366	104—Winchester to Langdon.
17	891	77—Cherbourg to Ryde.
18	1162	140—Cherbourg to Norwood.

Total..19,067

By adding the velocities in these races together, and then dividing by the number of races (18), we obtain an average velocity of 1059 yards per minute, which, omitting fractions is equivalent to 36 miles an hour.

The fastest race chronicled in the above table is No. 3, from Ventnor to Manchester, in which a velocity of about fifty-five miles an hour was maintained for four hours in succession, but then the weather was clear, and wind favourable, being south-west.

The slowest race in the list was No. 5, in which the winning bird only accomplished 443 yards per minute ; but this was so exceptionally slow a flight, that there must have been a disturbing cause, as many of the best birds in the kingdom competed : and from Granville (No. 7), three weeks after, the same birds more than doubled the rate of travelling, and a fortnight later some of them came from Rennes (No. 8) with nearly treble the speed of the race from Ventnor, although the distance was two and a half times greater.

When it is thus demonstrated that the average rate of speed of the fastest trained pigeons, *la créme de la créme*—the picked birds of thousands—is under forty miles an hour, and that even with a favourable wind it does not reach sixty, the crudity of the opinions often hazarded as to the rate of flight of game birds becomes evident.

It is much easier to gain a correct idea of the comparative speed of other birds with that of pigeons than to arrive at an independent conclusion from seeing them fly. When a partridge is in the air we cannot accurately gauge his rate of flight ; but knowing that the average rate of flight of a pigeon is under forty miles an hour, we can make an approximation as to the speed of other birds.

W. B. Tegetmeier.

o

With game birds few experiments have been made ; but the following article, from the *Field* of Feb. 19, 1887, gives particulars of some chronographic experiments carried out with partridges and pheasants as well as pigeons. In these instances the birds were neither aided nor retarded by the wind, as the day was perfectly calm. The difference between the best pigeons in these experiments, and the average of the races given above, was not very great ; and the pheasants were a trifle faster than the pigeons, especially in the open, while the partridges were not quite so fast.

EXPERIMENTS TO ASCERTAIN THE VELOCITY OF FLIGHT OF BIRDS.

The rate of speed attained by birds that are commonly shot by sportsmen has been the subject of a good deal of discussion in the *Field*, and very conflicting opinions have been expressed with respect to their powers of flight. In order, if possible, to obtain data of a more reliable character than many vague surmises which have been indulged in, we requested the assistance of Mr. Griffith, who has from time to time furnished our readers with so much valuable information relative to the velocities of shot and the explosive force of gunpowders ; and he not only very kindly complied with our request, but has improved upon the method we suggested for carrying out the experiments.

The series ot trials was commenced with pigeons, which it was thought might probably be more amenable than wild game to the conditions connected with their flight, and so, in the event of there being any hitch in the arrangements, there would be a better chance for the apparatus to be got into thorough working order before attempting experiments with partridges or pheasants. In order to secure a good standard of comparison, Mr. Hammond, the well-known purveyor of pigeons for the Hurlingham Club, was asked to select some of his very best " blue rocks " to pass through the ordeal. The experiments with these birds were carried out about two months ago, on a fine clear day in the middle of December, when there was no wind whatever to enhance or diminish the natural speed of the birds.

The pigeons commenced their flight at one end of the covered range, or experimental shooting gallery, of the Schultze Gunpowder Company, in the New Forest, and the birds thus had the opportunity of getting well on the wing before they reached the other extremity, where was placed the apparatus employed to record their rate of speed after they had flown 40 yards. Two " screens," or arrangements of fine threads, were here put into connection with the electric apparatus, and through these threads the birds must necessarily dash in their flight, in order to make their exit from the range. The so-called " screens " were composed of the finest invisible-grey cotton, so easily broken as not to check the flight of the birds in the slightest degree, and the successive breakages were instantaneously recorded by the electrical apparatus. Between the two screens there was an intervening space of 6ft. 9in. (a distance which was adopted from its being convenient for regulating the chronograph), and, the apparatus having recorded the time taken by the bird in traversing this $2\frac{1}{4}$ yards interval, the velocity was then readily convertible into yards per second or miles per hour.

In order that the birds might fly directly towards these screens all apertures in the building were darkened except the open end of the range ; and, as the birds, on being liberated, would naturally fly towards the broad daylight, and be likely to gain full confidence as they approached the place of exit, it was hoped that each of them might be led to do its best by the time it reached the point where the record of speed was to be made. The results, on the whole, were very satisfactory. Now and then a bird would not fly straight, or would check its flight before dashing through the screens ; but, whenever such was the case, the record was rejected as defective, and accordingly does not figure in the list which is given below. The number of good flights, however, was sufficient to enable Mr. Griffith to make twelve fair records of speed, the particulars of which are as follows :

PIGEONS IN THE 40 YARDS' RANGE.	TIME. Seconds.	RATE OF SPEED.	
		Yards per Second.	Miles per Hour.
1st	·157	14·3	29·3
2nd	·156	14·4	29·5
3rd	·168	13·4	27·4
4th	·150	15·0	30·7
5th	·163	13·8	28·2
6th	·139	16·2	33·1
7th	·169	13·3	27·2
8th	·153	14·7	30·1
9th	·168	13·4	27·4
10th	·176	12·8	26·1
11th	·157	14·3	29·3
12th	·136	16·5	33·8

Having obtained the above chronographic results in the covered range, Mr. Griffith was not content to let matters end there, and he therefore determined to place these velocities in comparison with records of flight in the open. For this purpose he adopted a method very similar to that which has

since been suggested by "Vivarii Custos" (*Field*, Jan. 15) as
a means of ascertaining the flight of driven partridges. Mr.
Griffith placed men in ambush at various measured distances,
with instructions to signal as soon as a bird arrived opposite
either of the stations. When the bird had flown 25 yards from
the starting point in the open, the time was taken by means of
a stop watch, and the record was completed as soon as the
signal was given of the bird having accomplished either of the
measured distances. In four instances the birds went straight
away, and the records were as under :

		RATE OF SPEED.	
FLIGHT OF PIGEONS IN THE OPEN.	TIME. Seconds.	Yards per Second.	Miles per Hour.
240 yards	19	12·6	25·8
265 ,, ...	20	13·2	27·0
300 ,, ...	22	13·6	27·9
132 ,, ...	10	13·2	27·0

With reference to these results Mr. Griffith says : "I
expected the free long flight would beat the chronograph velocities
at 40 yards, but the reverse is the case. I imagine the reason
is, that when started from a trap or basket, as these were, the
birds fly in alarm at first, but when away in the open they do
not keep up their full pace." In neither case, however, did
these "blue rocks" come up to the average speed of the
trained "homing birds" of which Mr. Tegetmeier gave particulars in the *Field* of the 22nd ult. There the average speed of
the winning birds in eighteen pigeon races amounted to 36
miles an hour—the highest velocity, with a favourable wind,
being at the rate of 55 miles an hour. In Mr. Griffith's experiments the highest velocity was nearly 34 miles an hour, without
any wind whatever.

Mr. Griffith's next task was to try similar experiments with partridges and pheasants, and for that purpose it was desirable to obtain a supply of good wild birds, as those kept in confinement could not be taken as fair representatives of the power of flight of birds which had always been at liberty. The difficulty, however, for many weeks, was to get such specimens as were wanted, the snow upon the ground and other circumstances being unfavourable to their capture. At length, however, some birds were obtained, all very wild and active, and last week Mr. Griffith proceeded with his experiments.

The conditions as to screens, &c., were as previously stated. Some of the pheasants were inveterate runners and would not rise to the screens at all; others rose fairly, but they did not all of them exhibit an equal degree of earnestness, and the best six records obtained were as follows, the first being that of a splendid bird, who went through the screens in fine style. The respective times and velocities are as follows :

| | | RATE OF SPEED. | |
PHEASANTS IN THE 40 YARDS' RANGE.	TIME. Seconds.	Yards per Second.	Miles per Hour.
1st	·136	16·5	33·8
2nd	·156	14·4	29·5
3rd	·186	12·1	24·7
4th	·189	11·9	24·4
5th	·225	10·0	20·5
6th	·139	16·2	33·1

Some of the birds were also timed in the open, and, as on the day of the previous experiments, there was no wind whatever. Two of the pheasants went away straight at fine speed; a third doubled back, and is therefore omitted from the record ; and the fourth went straight away, but with much less velocity than the first two. From the following records it will be seen that, contrary to the experience with the " blue rocks," the pheasants attained their highest speed in the open :

FLIGHT OF PHEASANTS IN THE OPEN.	TIME. Seconds.	RATE OF SPEED.	
		Yards per Second.	Miles per Hour.
265 yards ...	15·0	17·7	36·1
220 ,, ...	11·8	18·6	38·1
140 ,, ...	10·6	13·2	27·0

The concluding experiment was with the partridges, which went fairly well at the screens, though they did not seem to exert themselves very much ; and the following were the records obtained :

PARTRIDGES IN THE 40 YARDS' RANGE.	TIME. Seconds.	RATE OF SPEED.	
		Yards per Second.	Miles per Hour.
1st	·172	13·1	26·8
2nd	·188	12·0	24·5
3rd	·194	11·6	23·7
4th	·162	13·9	28·4

Here, in the range, the partridges did not fly so fast as the " blue rocks " ; but they did better in the open, so far as the records go. Only two of them, however, flew far enough to have their time recorded. The rest dropped to the ground before they got to the men who were stationed to signal their arrival. The speed of these two were as follows :

FLIGHT OF PARTRIDGES IN THE OPEN.	TIME. Seconds.	RATE OF SPEED.	
		Yards per Second.	Miles per Hour.
170 yards ...	12·6	13·5	27·6
220 ,, ...	14·0	15·7	32·1

Mr. Griffith says, in conclusion : " I think the velocities may be fairly taken as the speed of birds rising to the gun, and also of driven game when not aided by any wind."

Of course, when driven birds are going down wind with all the advantage of a strong breeze, the velocity of the wind has to be added to the natural speed of the bird. In order to afford an idea of the amount of assistance that would be rendered to birds flying down wind, a short table of velocities may be given. A wind moving at the rate of three or four miles an hour is scarcely perceptible ; and other gradations in miles per hour, and feet per second, are as follows :

	Miles. per Hour.	Feet per Second.		Miles per Hour	Feet. per Second.
Gentle air	7	10·25	Gale	40	58·68
Light breeze	14	20·50	Heavy storm	60	88·0
Steady breeze	21	30·75	Hurricane	80	117·36

It will be seen that a mile per hour is just about equivalent to 1½ feet per second.

PENETRATION OF SHOT AT "TALL" PHEASANTS.

[*I am indebted to Mr. W. W. WATTS and the Proprietors of "THE FIELD" for permission to publish the following, extracted from "THE FIELD," December 18th, 1897.*]

SIR,—As many experienced shots are under the impression that pheasants 40 yards high are out of the killing range of ordinary sporting guns, I have carried out the experiment as detailed below, with a view to ascertaining whether any difference in penetration of shot fired vertically, as against the same fired horizontally, does exist.

I had some difficulty in finding a suitable elevation, but Mr. Alfred Richards came to my rescue, and, through his neighbour, Mr. Neive, obtained for me access to one of the highest windmills in Norfolk. I have also to thank Mr. Moore, who, in the interest of sport, stopped his mill for nearly a whole day.

The box hanging from the top of the poles lashed to the uppermost sail was exactly 120 ft. from the ground—the measure being taken with a plumb line suspended from it, which also guided my aim. The said box had an aperture at its bottom end of 8 in. by 3 in., which was filled by a strawboard, and succeeding ones continued every ¾ in. up to twenty-four.

Five shots were fired and the result noted, and then the box was lowered and placed 40 measured yards distant to receive five horizontal shots. The results were as follows :

VERTICAL TEST.			HORIZONTAL TEST.		
Pellets through 18 strawboards... ...	1		Pellets through 22 strawboards... ...	1	
,, ,, 17 ,, ...	2		,, ,, 18 ,, ...	1	
,, ,, 15 ,, ...	10		,, ,, 17 ,, ...	3	
,, ,, 14 ,, ...	5		,, ,, 16 ,, ...	2	
,, ,, 13 ,, ...	5		,, ,, 15 ,, ...	5	
,, ,, 12 ,, ...	2		,, ,, 14 ,, ...	6	
,, ,, 11 ,, ...	1		,, ,, 13 ,, ...	4	
Average penetration, 14·31.			,, ,, 12 ,, ...	2	
			,, ,, 11 ,, ...	3	
			,, ,, 10 ,, ...	1	
			Average penetration, 14·46.		

The right barrel of a good 12-bore was used, which makes a pattern of about 140, and the load was 42 grs. Schultze and 1⅛ oz. No. 6 Walker's hard shot.

The shooting was very even, the five shots of each series producing nearly an equal number of hits (viz., 26 pellets in the vertical rounds, and 28 in the horizontal). On referring to the figures it will be seen that the bulk of the pellets stopped after penetrating 13, 14, and 15 cards, and the average result is practically the same in each case.

A very aged and noted wildfowler of the Broads witnessed the trial, and he was confident the vertical penetration would be weak, from the observations he had made in large numbers of practical experiments on fowl with his long single muzzle-loader by Egg.

This experience points to the fact that birds overhead appear nearer than they really are ; or, if this is not so, the difficulties of judging where and how to fire in front are intensified at this angle.

W. W. WATTS.

[Mr. Watt's experiments, as described above, appear to us to thoroughly confirm the theoretical conclusions on this subject—viz., that there would be no practical difference in the penetration of the shot at the height of 40 yards, from that given at the same distance when fired horizontally. Theoretically there would be a slight amount of difference, owing to the "gravity pull;" but the time of the shot in traversing 40 yards is only about one-seventh of a second, and in that interval of time the influence of gravity would lessen the height of the shot by the 49th part of 16 feet —*i.e.*, about four inches ; so that firing vertically at a target placed at the height of 40 yards would be equivalent to firing horizontally at one placed at a distance of 40 yards 4 inches.—ED.]

(See Illustration on next page).

The sketch herewith will illustrate how the trial was conducted:

PENETRATION CARD RACK ATTACHED TO SAIL OF WINDMILL.

VARIATIONS IN PATTERN OF GUNS.

From the *Field*, November 17th, 1894.

SIR,—I should be much obliged if you or some of your readers would kindly give me their opinion as to whether the following is a good performance for pattern for a 12-bore modified choke gun, averaging about 170 pellets in a 30in. circle on a target at 40 yards, when charged with 42grs. of Schultze powder, and 1⅛oz. of No. 6 shot (270 to ounce). The pellets are, as a rule, spread sufficiently closely and evenly throughout the 30in. circle (with the exception of two or three gaps, which seem always to occur) to prevent a partridge escaping through it; but every now and then (perhaps once in ten or twelve shots) the circle contains only about 80 or 100 pellets so irregularly spread that a bird could escape almost anywhere in it.

Now I am inclined to think that in the very best guns, whether chokes or cylinders, such a bad and erratic pattern as I have just described will occasionally occur, and cannot be accounted for. Moreover, I should say that no 12-bore gun, loaded with the above charge, can be counted upon, as a general rule, to spread its pellets so closely and evenly as to avoid leaving any gaps which would let a partridge through in the so-called killing circle. But I should very much like to hear the experience of others on the above points.   WHIMBREL.

[If our correspondent will refer to the records we have recently published, he will see that, in half a dozen successive rounds, one or more instances frequently occur in which the pattern is considerably below the average, although the cartridges for these experiments are loaded with an exceptional amount of care. There are also wide variations in velocity, recoil and strain in the barrel. Whether the differences result from variations in the strength of the caps, we cannot say with certainty, but we think it very probable. Generally speaking, the black powders are less susceptible to such differences than are the nitro powders, as will be seen by referring to an article on "Standard Records with the 12-bore," in the *Field* of Sept. 29th last. With No. 2 black powder the patterns varied from 160 to 180, the average being 174; of six rounds with No. 4 black, the lowest pattern was 120 and the highest 187—the average being 164; and with some of the nitro powders the differences were still greater.—ED.]

204

TABLE OF PROPORTIONAL PATTERNS.

Shooting of gun as shown by percentage of charge in 30 in. circle at 40 yards.	Weight of charge in oz.	Pellets in 30 in. circle at 40 yds. for different sizes of shot.						
		3	4	5	5½	6	6½	7
80 %	1¼	140	172	218	240	272	300	340
	1⅛	126	155	196	216	**243**	270	306
	1 1/16	119	146	186	204	230	255	289
	1	112	138	174	192	216	240	272
	15/16	105	129	163	180	202	225	255
	⅞	98	121	153	168	189	210	238
	13/16	91	112	142	156	175	195	221
75 % FULL-CHOKE. (70 to 75 %)	1¼	131	161	205	225	254	281	319
	1⅛	119	146	184	203	**228**	254	287
	1 1/16	112	137	174	191	215	239	271
	1	105	129	164	180	203	225	255
	15/16	98	121	153	169	190	211	239
	⅞	92	113	143	158	177	197	224
	13/16	86	105	133	146	164	183	207
70 %	1¼	123	151	191	210	237	263	298
	1⅛	111	136	172	189	**213**	237	268
	1 1/16	104	128	162	179	201	223	253
	1	98	120	153	168	189	210	238
	15/16	92	113	143	158	177	197	223
	⅞	86	106	134	147	165	184	209
	13/16	80	98	124	137	153	171	193
65 %	1¼	114	140	177	195	220	244	276
	1⅛	103	126	159	176	**198**	220	249
	1 1/16	97	119	151	166	187	207	235
	1	91	112	142	156	176	195	221
	15/16	85	105	133	146	164	183	207
	⅞	80	98	124	137	153	171	194
	13/16	74	91	115	127	142	159	179
60 % HALF-CHOKE. (55 to 60 %)	1¼	105	129	164	180	203	225	255
	1⅛	95	116	147	162	**182**	203	230
	1 1/16	89	110	139	153	172	191	217
	1	84	103	131	144	162	180	204
	15/16	79	97	122	135	152	169	191
	⅞	74	91	115	126	142	158	179
	13/16	68	84	106	117	131	146	166

The Patterns obtained with 1⅛oz. of No. 6 shot are shown in black figures.

TABLE OF PROPORTIONAL PATTERNS—*continued.*

Shooting of gun as shown by percentage of charge in 30in. circle at 40 yards.	Weight of charge in oz.	Pellets in 30 in. circle at 40 yds. for different sizes of shot.						
		3	**4**	**5**	**5½**	**6**	**6½**	**7**
	1¼	96	118	150	165	186	206	234
	1⅛	87	107	135	149	**167**	186	211
	1 1/16	82	101	128	140	158	175	199
55 %	1	77	95	120	132	149	165	187
	15/16	72	89	112	124	139	155	175
	7/8	68	83	105	116	130	145	164
	13/16	63	77	97	107	120	134	152
	1¼	88	108	137	150	169	188	213
	1⅛	79	97	123	135	**152**	169	192
	1 1/16	75	92	116	128	144	160	181
50 %	1	70	86	109	120	135	150	170
	15/16	66	81	102	113	127	141	160
	7/8	62	76	96	105	118	132	149
	13/16	57	70	89	98	110	122	138
	1¼	79	97	123	135	152	169	191
	1⅛	71	87	110	122	**137**	152	172
45 % IMPROVED CYLINDER.	1 1/16	67	82	104	115	129	144	162
	1	63	77	98	108	122	135	153
	15/16	59	72	92	101	114	126	144
	7/8	55	68	86	95	106	118	134
	13/16	51	63	80	88	99	110	124
	1¼	70	86	109	120	135	150	170
	1⅛	63	78	98	108	**122**	135	153
	1 1/16	60	73	93	102	115	128	144
40 %	1	56	69	87	96	108	120	136
	15/16	52	64	82	90	101	112	128
	7/8	49	60	76	84	94	105	119
	13/16	46	56	71	78	88	98	110
	1¼	61	75	96	105	118	131	149
	1⅛	55	68	86	95	**106**	118	134
35 % TRUE CYLINDER.	1 1/16	52	64	81	89	100	112	126
	1	49	60	76	84	95	105	119
	15/16	46	56	71	79	89	98	112
	7/8	43	53	67	74	83	92	104
	13/16	40	49	62	68	77	85	97

The Patterns obtained with 1⅛oz. of No. 6 shot are shown in black figures. From " Notes on Shooting."

SPREAD OF SHOT FROM GUNS OF DIFFERENT GAUGES.

Many are, no doubt, under the impression that 16, 20, and 28-bore guns will shoot their respective charges closer than the usual 12, and that they are harder shooting guns under those circumstances. I have never found this the case; and, in support of my opinion, insert the following letter, with editorial remarks, from the *Field* of the 22nd December, 1888, which fully endorse it :—

Sir,—I observe that your able correspondent "Purple Heather," in the *Field* of the 15th inst., distinctly asserts that with 1 oz. of No. 6 shot a 20 or a 16-bore will not shoot closer than a 12. It would be interesting to know whether this is an absolutely reliable and thoroughly ascertained fact ; for it is entirely contrary to the general opinion on the subject.

It constantly happens that a man, finding his shooting unsatisfactory with a 16-bore, and believing himself not to be a sufficiently good shot to use such a close-shooting gun, straightway discards the 16-bore, and provides himself with a 12, in the hope that his shooting may thereby improve. Whether his hopes are generally or ever realised may be quite another matter. Perhaps I may be allowed to relate my own experience on this point. It will be found in one respect to support the assertion of a "Purple Heather."

I am what may be called an indifferent shot—that is to say, though I manage to bag a good deal of game in a day's shooting, still I very often miss astonishingly easy shots. I have always been in the habit of shooting with a 16-bore, made by a first-class London gun-maker. However, last season some of my relations and friends strongly advised me to try a 12-bore—my gun-maker also gave me the same advice—all holding the opinion that only a very good shot should use a 16-bore, as it carried so close as greatly to increase the chance of missing the object aimed at. I allowed myself to be persuaded by such apparently cogent reasoning, and have shot with a 12-bore all through this season. The result has been most disappointing. I have not shot nearly so well as I did with the 16, and have had the trouble of carrying a heavier weapon (6¾ lb.).

I am sorry I changed, but, before discarding my 12 and resuming my 16-bore, I intend to persevere a little longer, and load with only 1 oz. of shot instead of 1⅛ oz., which, up to the present time, I have been using. I may add that both my guns are by the same maker, and fit me most accurately, the right barrel in each gun being non-choke, and the left modified choke.

So far, therefore, I am inclined to agree with " Purple Heather," and believe that an average shot is likely to shoot every bit as well with a 16-bore as with a 12.   TIREUR.

[It appears to us that the spread of the pellets depends not so much upon the size of the bore as on the nature of the boring. Whatever may have been the case in the pre-choke-bore period, the results of experiments with choked barrels go to show that, with equal charges of shot, the patterns of the small-bores are not closer than those of guns of larger gauge. In the *Field* Gun Trial of 1879, there were twenty-three guns loaded with equal charges of shot (1 oz.), eleven of these guns being 20-bores, eleven 16-bores, and one 12-bore. The patterns of the 20-bores averaged 147, those of the 16-bores averaged 162, and that of the 12-bore was 183. Again, in our issue of April 14 last, particulars were published of the trial of a 24-bore gun and a light 12-bore, with equal charges of powder and shot ; the 24-bore gave 154 pattern, and the 12-bore 200. And a few weeks ago another trial took place (*Field*, Nov. 10), in which the charges were not equal, but of the quantities that were used the 28-bore put 68 per cent. in the 30-in. circle, the 24-bore put in 69 per cent., and the 12-bore 71 per cent. But these were choke-bores. With the average 12-bore cylinder gun, the portion of the charge put in the target at 40 yards is only 40 per cent., the remaining 60 per cent. being outside the 30-in. circle ; and it seems probable, from what he states, that such a gun would suit " Tireur " better than a choke-bore.—ED.]

Scoring a Right and Left with Lancaster Game Scorer.

THE LANCASTER GAME SCORER.

(*From the Press.*)

A very simple, yet ingenious, game marker has just been introduced into the sporting world by Mr. Charles Lancaster, and there can be no doubt whatever but that it will speedily become very popular. Many markers have been invented from time to time, with more or less success, but this new one (*see Ill.* No. 68, page 209) is calculated to outrival all its

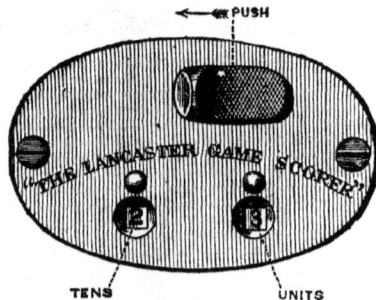

predecessors, and become recognised as the marker *par excellence.* The first illustration we give is the exact size of the scorer, and from it anyone can readily see the working of it. We also give a second illustration, showing the scorer as attached to the gun stock. Very little wood indeed has to be removed from the stock in order to fix the marker, so that those sportsmen who have guns with the stock after the pattern of Turner's Featherweight, &c., can easily have it fixed to their guns ; and another item to which special attention has been given in designing it, is to construct it in such a manner that it may go on the side instead of being let in the top of the stock. As the working parts are made of

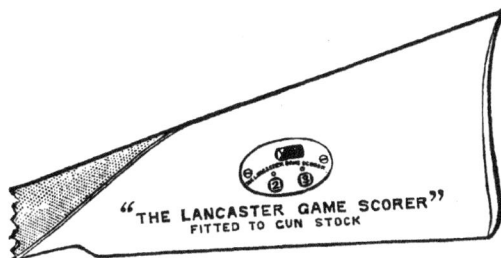

"THE LANCASTER GAME SCORER"
FITTED TO GUN STOCK

brass, there is no reason to fear they will be affected by rust; and, again, the whole thing is so light that the balance of the gun is in no way interfered with.

The manipulation of the marker is exceedingly simple (*see Ill.*) The slide is pushed forward by the thumb, and this movement does not require the hand to support the stock in the act of pressing, so as to insure the full movement of the thumb-piece. When the slide is pushed forward, the numbered wheel with the units turns round one number (giving a click in doing so), and when it has moved from 0 to 9 the second wheel, with the tens, is brought into contact, and caused by the same push to rotate one figure at the same time as the unit wheel brings the 0 into view. The same process of nine registrations has then again to be gone through before the decimal wheel is again brought into contact, and in this manner 109 may be registered before it is necessary to commence over again.

MEMORANDA.

SHOT—SIZES AND NUMBER OF PELLETS PER OZ., AVDP.

NEWCASTLE.		WALKERS, PARKER & CO., LIMITED, LONDON.			
		PATENT.		HARD.	
A A A	.. 40	A A A	 36	A A A	.. 36
A A	.. 48	A A	 41	A A	.. 41
A	.. 56	A	 44	A	.. 44
B B B B	.. 56	—	—	—	—
B B B	.. 64	B B B	 51	B B B	.. 51
B B	.. 76	B B	 55	B B	.. 57
B	.. 88	B	 64	B	.. 66
1	.. 104	1	 79	1	.. 80
2	.. 122	2	 96	2	.. 98
3	.. 140	3	 119	3	.. 120
4	.. 172	4	 173	4	.. 180
5	.. 218	5	 220	5	.. 220
6	.. 270	*6	 268	6	.. 270
7	.. 340	7	 345	7	.. 345
8	.. 450	8	 450	8	.. 450
9	.. 580	smaller sizes not by count.			
10	.. 850				

* CHARLES LANCASTER'S special size of shot, "Medium Game" 240 to oz., is the best for all Shootings.

SHOT—NUMBER OF PELLETS IN A CHARGE.

(OF NEWCASTLE MANUFACTURE.)

Nos.	¾ oz.	⅞ oz.	1 oz.	1⅛ oz.	1¼ oz.	Relative Number of Pellets.	Relative Weight (=Striking Force) of the Pellets.
3	105	122	140	157	175	1·000	1·000
4	129	150	172	193	215	1·229	0·814
5	163	191	218	245	272	1·555	0·642
6	202	236	270	304	338	1·929	0·519
7	255	297	340	382	425	2·429	0·412
8	334	394	450	506	562	3·214	0·311

WEIGHTS OF POWDER CHARGES.

IN DRACHMS, GRAINS AND GRAMMES.

1	Drachm =	27·34	Grains =	1·772	Grammes.
2	,,	54·6	,,	3·54	,,
2⅛	,,	58·1	,,	3·76	,,
2¼	,,	61·5	,,	3·98	,,
2⅜	,,	64·9	,,	4·20	,,
2½	,,	68·3	,,	4·42	,,
2⅝	,,	71·8	,,	4·64	,,
2¾	,,	75·2	,,	4·87	,,
2⅞	,,	78·6	,,	5·09	,,
3	,,	82·0	,,	5·32	,,
3⅛	,,	85·4	,,	5·54	,,
3¼	,,	88·9	,,	5·76	,,

LEGAL SEASONS for KILLING GAME, &c.

Kinds of Game.	England and Wales.		Scotland.		Ireland.	
	Begins.	Ends.	Begins.	Ends.	Begins.	Ends.
Grouse or Moor Fowl ..	Aug. 12	Dec. 10	Aug. 12	Dec. 10	Aug. 12	Dec. 10
Blackgame or Heath Fowl	Aug. 20*	Dec. 10	Aug. 20	Dec. 10	Aug. 20	Dec. 10
Ptarmigan	No clos	e season	Aug. 12	Dec. 10	..	..
Partridge	Sept. 1	Feb. 1	Sept. 1	Feb. 1	Sept. 20	Jan. 10
Pheasant..	Oct. 1	Feb. 1	Oct. 1	Feb. 1	Oct. 1	Feb. 1
Quail	As Wild	Birds	As Wild	Birds	Sept. 20	Jan. 10
Landrail	ditto	ditto	ditto	ditto	Sept. 20	Jan. 10
Bustard	Sept. 1	March 1	ditto	ditto	Sept. 1	Jan. 10
Hare	No clos	e season	No clos	e season	Aug. 12	April 20
Male Fallow Deer	ditto	ditto	ditto	ditto	June 10	Sept. 29
Other Male Deer	ditto	ditto	ditto	ditto	June 10	Dec. 31
Wildfowl and other birds not game†	Aug. 1	March 1	Aug. 1	March 1	Aug. 1	March 1

* Except in Somerset, Devon, and the New Forest, where the commencement of black game shooting is deferred until September 1st.

† On the application of the local authorities, the Secretary of State in England and Wales, the Secretary for Scotland in Scotland, or the Lord Lieutenant in Ireland, has power to vary or abolish the close time for any bird or birds in any county by order to be published in the *Gazette*. These various powers have been exercised in many cases.

Quail, landrail, woodcock, and snipe, cannot legally be shot without a game licence.

It is unlawful to kill pheasants, partridges, grouse, moorgame, or hares, on a Sunday or Christmas Day.

The close time for hares *in Ireland* ranges *from* March 1st in co. Limerick, and April 1st, in the majority of cases, *to* August 12th all over Ireland. The close season is fixed by the Lord Lieutenant on the application of the Grand Juries in the various counties.

Although there is no close time for hares in England during which they may not be killed, except on Sundays and Christmas Day, it is illegal *to sell* or expose for sale any hare during the months of March, April, May, June and July, under the Hares Preservation Act of 1892 (55 and 56 Vict. c. 8), unless they are " foreign hares " imported into Great Britain (sec. 3).

(From " The Field Sports Protection and Encouragement Association.")

GUN LICENCES.

	£	s.	d.
LICENCE (ANNUAL) TO USE OR CARRY A GUN :—			
To expire 31st July..	0	10	0
LICENCE TO SHOOT GAME :—			
If taken out after 31st July, and before 1st November, to expire 31st July following	3	0	0
After 31st July, to expire 31st October following	2	0	0
After 31st October, to expire 31st July following	2	0	0
For a continuous period of Fourteen days	1	0	0
GAMEKEEPERS (GREAT BRITAIN) :—			
To expire 31st July..	2	0	0

A Licence to kill Game covers a Gun Licence.

WEIGHTS OF SOME GAME BIRDS, ETC.

For purposes of reference it is useful to have a table of the weights of the more common game birds and animals that are shot. With that object in view I have inserted the following :—

Capercaillie .. .. 11lbs. to 13lbs.	European woodcock 12 ozs. to 14ozs.
Black game .. .. 3¼ ,, 3½ ,,	Great, or full snipe 7 ,, 9 ,,
Red grouse (Scotch) 1¼ ,, 1¾ ,,	Common ,, 4 ,, 5 ,,
Pheasant (cock) .. 2½ ,, 3½ ,,	Jack ,, 2 ,, 2¼ ,,
,, (hen) .. 2¼ ,, 3 ,,	Hare .. .. .. 7 lbs. to 9 lbs.
Grey or " English "	Rabbit .. .. ..2½ ,, 3¼ ,,
partridge .. .. 10 ozs. to 14ozs.	Wood pigeon .. ..1¼ ,, 1½ ,,
French partridge .. 15 ,, 1¼lbs.	

The above weights are those usually attained to by ordinary well-grown specimens, but it must not be forgotten that occasionally exceptional weights are recorded, much exceeding those given.

BOOKS ON SHOOTING.

CHARLES LANCASTER begs to draw the attention of his patrons to the following works, copies of which every sportsman should have in his library :—

"The Dead Shot, or Sportsman's Complete Guide." By "Marksman."

"Shooting." The Badminton Library. 2 vols. By Lord Walsingham and Sir Ralph Payne-Gallwey, Bart.

"Letters to Young Shooters." By Sir Ralph Payne-Gallwey, Bart.

"Fur and Feather Series." Edited by Alfred E. T. Watson.
Published by Longmans, Green & Co., London.

"Something about Guns & Shooting." By "Purple Heather."
Published by Alexander & Shepheard, London.

"Practical Wildfowling." By Hy. Sharp.
Published by L. Upcott Gill, London.

"The Modern Sportsman's Gun and Rifle." 2 vols. By the late J. H. Walsh ("Stonehenge"), Editor of the *Field*.
Published by Horace Cox, London.

"Notes on Shooting," with instructions concerning the use of Black Gunpowder. By an Old Manufacturer.
Published by Curtis's & Harvey, London.

Also

"A Primer of Explosives." By Major A. Cooper-Key (1905).

CORRESPONDENCE ON DEFECTIVE SHOOTING.

The following Letter appeared in the *Field*:—

10th December, 1887.

SIR,—I notice a letter in the *Field* of last Saturday, signed H. H. N., asking if any of your correspondents can recommend a "good professor" to teach the art of shooting, &c. I strongly advise H. H. N. to pay a visit to Mr. Charles Lancaster, of 151, New Bond Street.* I myself have learnt many valuable hints from him, and I have taken several friends of mine (who were, I may say, real "duffers") to him, and they have all blessed me and their "professor," inasmuch as they can now make very respectable bags. The fact is, that Mr. C. Lancaster is not only an excellent and painstaking "coach," but he understands better than any gun-maker I have come across how to fit a man properly with a gun. I notice H. H. N. asks particularly about fit. Of course, the sportsman himself must state weight of gun he can conveniently wield during a long day's tramp. This is a very important question, as I have lately discovered.

I may mention one fact, which will, I think, show that Mr. Lancaster can assist in the art of shooting. I met Miss Annie Oakley the first day she shot at his private grounds, and I was also present when she first came to our club ground (the Gun Club). At this period Miss Oakley could kill about one blue rock out of five. After Mr. Lancaster had finished his course of instruction she killed forty-one rocks out of fifty, and for this performance she selected her Lancaster 20-bores—a pair of beautiful guns built for exhibition shooting—in preference to her Lancaster 12's. Miss A. Oakley had previously told me that "her ambition was to kill thirty-five blue rocks out of fifty before she left England."

PURPLE HEATHER.

* Now removed to 11, Panton Street, Haymarket.

5th January, 1889.

SIR,—Your correspondent "Duffer," in his letter in your issue of the 8th December, headed "Improvement of Defective Shooting," asked how I proceeded in order to improve my shooting. I could not reply to that question in few words, as it took me a long time to work out the answer to the riddle ; but, speaking generally, I may say that the causes which give rise to bad shooting cover an extremely wide ground. They are certainly not to be compressed within the limits of a single letter ; and without a previous knowledge of the individual and his surroundings, I should as little think of venturing to account (even were I a professed teacher in the art of shooting, which, be it distinctly understood, I am not) for defects of workmanship in a particular case, as I should attempt to give a rational answer to the inquiry, which from time to time appears in papers devoted to the interests of ladies, "Why do my servants lie in bed so late of a morning ? "

I have, however, been asked a direct question, viz., "What gun-maker has successfully fitted me ? " That I can answer. It was Mr. Charles Lancaster. I one day saw a letter in the *Field*, stating that Mr. C. Lancaster was an adept at fitting a customer with a gun. I forget who wrote it, but after my sorry experiences you may readily believe that I perused it with avidity. I had no previous personal knowledge of Mr. C. Lancaster, but I forthwith determined to make his acquaintance. Now, I am not such a fool as to say that Mr. Charles Lancaster is the only gun-maker in the world who can properly fit a man with a gun. I will simply tell some of your inquiring correspondents what he did for me.

I had been using a gun with which I could shoot, if I do not say really well, at all events with the greatest " condence " and comfort. I have an abhorrence of talking about

"how many head I killed in how many shots," and I am
not keen on purchasing a "Gallwey Game Marker," or a
"Lancaster Game Scorer," as I rarely count the pheasants,
rabbits, hares, &c., that I bag, strange though it may seem
to admit such an error ; still, I may say that with my old
favourite gun I do remember that I have frequently in
covert shooting killed twenty-five head out of twenty-eight
shots ; at times I have bagged five-and-forty head in fifty
shots. These instances are, of course, rare. I was never
one of your "never miss gentlemen." My motto is "shoot
liberally and don't pick your shots." I merely mention the
above facts in order to show that I had some reason for
alarm when, with my new guns I found myself bagging five,
ten, or fifteen head out of forty or fifty shots. I knew and
felt I ought to do better. Many and many a time I have
been told that a "good workman does not complain of his
tools." Still I went on in my own way, and at last got hold
of a gun that did suit me.

After trying choke-bores, cylinders, heavy guns, light
guns, short stocks, long stocks, 30in. barrels, 28in. barrels,
guns heavy forward, then the reverse, I called one day upon
Mr. C. Lancaster, and overwhelmed him with facts of what
I could do, and could not do (I admit it was principally of
what I could *not* do) ; at all events I was "exuberant with
my own verbosity," and eventually I wound up almost
breathless with the words, "Do you think you can fit me
with a gun ? "—" I have no pattern for you "—" I have
lost my favourite gun." Mr. Lancaster is not a man of
many words. He did not say, "Oh, yes ; I can fit you
splendidly ; " he said "I should prefer first to make you
a plain gun, which you can try, and then we can alter it if
necessary ; you can then decide whether you prefer to keep
it or have a best quality gun." I saw, however, by his quiet

businesslike manner that he knew what he was about. I
told Mr. Lancaster that I had been accustomed to a stock
of evidently somewhat unusual and old-fashioned shape,
and when I threw a trial gun or two up to the shoulder,
while he was standing at my side, I did my level best to put
them up as I would when in the field (though this is difficult
to do), and he made his notes. In due time I received the
new gun, and I can honestly say a complete metamorphosis
took place in my shooting. In my first trial trip (I happened
to get an invitation to stay with a friend who had a little
piece of shooting; he said, " Bring your gun, as you may
get a shot at a pheasant ; " and so I took it) I had thirteen
shots. I did take notice of what I killed the first few times
I went out with my new weapon, for obvious reasons, and I
bagged in a couple of hours eight pheasants, two hares, and
two rabbits—a nice pretty little mixed bag for about a couple
of hundred acres of shooting, late in the year.

I will not weary your readers with my successive ex-
ploits ; but I got on so well that I have had four guns of
Mr. Lancaster since my first trial one, and I really do not
think that I can speak too highly of what Mr. Lancaster has
done for me. In my own individual case I consider that
he has been extraordinarily successful. He has " picked
up " my shooting—well, what shall I say—50, or even 75,
per cent. ? And he had nothing to guide him. I think it
speaks volumes for his aptitude for fitting customers with
" a proper stock," as your correspondent wrote, and to him,
though I forget his name, I owe a deep debt of gratitude for
having put me on the right track.

Now, everyone " sticks " up for his own gun-maker, and,
as I have been asked the question " Who improved my
shooting ? " I have much pleasure in paying a just tribute
to my kind and painstaking gun-maker. Mr. Lancaster

gives lessons in shooting. I have not myself had any from him, though I have learnt many valuable hints when trying guns at his excellent private shooting grounds ; and, as I may be somewhat prejudiced in his favour, I would recommend your correspondents to get what I have said about his " fitting powers," " coaching ability," &c., verified by some of his pupils. I am sure he would send testimonials written by them to those of your subscribers who wished to see them.

Mr. C. Lancaster is now building me a new hammerless gun. I was once having a very prolonged conversation with my dear old friend " 20,000 Shots " on the subject of hammerless guns. You must know, Sir, that he and I have a battle-royal when we get together about " chokes and cylinders ; " but he is such an accomplished Sportsman, and such a fascinating man to talk to in so many ways, and so full of anecdote, that it is with the greatest difficulty that I can tear myself away from his company when we meet. Well, with reference to hammerless guns, " 20,000 Shots " said, " I prefer hammer guns ; but I suppose you must go with the time, and such being the case, you are safe in trying Mr. C. Lancaster's action." " 20,000 Shots " will, I daresay, remember the occasion to which I refer, when we kept his excellent wife waiting two hours for lunch ! But, Sir, you know what it is when Sportsmen or enthusiasts get together ! Some people have whispered " lunatics ! "

PURPLE HEATHER.

SIR,—I have to thank those gentlemen who have so kindly written to you in reply to " E. F. A. Y.'s " enquiries respecting my giving lessons in shooting, but I see your correspondent, " Another Failure," writes hoping that some expert in the use of the shot-gun would give practical hints on the art of shooting with a gun in a similar way as Sir Henry Halford had on the subject of rifle shooting, because he (and no doubt many others) could not avail themselves of my tuition, partly on account of expense, but really because of living at some distance from London.

I have, therefore, much pleasure in informing " Another Failure," through your columns, that as so many gentlemen have asked me to write a work, I have determined to compile a small " Treatise on the Art of Shooting," in which I shall do my best to produce an unpretentious little work, but, at the same time, collect the opinions of the highest authorities on the subject, together with hints, which I hope may be useful to many. The chief novelty will consist in a number of carefully executed diagrams, illustrating the best method of carrying out certain shots, whereby the novice may learn " angles," which are so essential for the making of an average, if not first-class shot.

CHARLES LANCASTER.

September, 1888.

P.S.—I shall be glad to receive suggestions from any of your readers who fancy they can, by doing so, improve the usefulness of the little work in question.

SIR,—I want to give an idea to our friend who wishes to improve, and it is one which does not seem to occur to him. Let him go out shooting quite alone, and if he finds an improvement he may have great hopes for himself. Many a man is made terribly nervous by shooting in a crowd, and being walked too fast. One dog alone to hunt up the birds, as a spaniel or terrier, which needs no control, is best. No one to mock the misses, not even a boy with him ; let him carry his own game, probably very little, and eat only what he bags. He will soon become a steady shot, I fancy, unless the sight is defective. If the above prescription is fairly tried, please to inform.

RED SETTER.

Sir,—As your correspondent, " E. F. A. Y." has not as yet had many answers concerning " Failure in Shooting," possibly I may be able to help him a little by giving what I consider to be the chief cause of bad shooting, arranged numerically according to their relative frequency of occurrence. I hope others of your readers will also give their opinions of the cause of misses which they have observed.

I should commence with the most common cause :—

1. Flurry at seeing and hearing game rise ; this leads to hurry, and

2. Carelessness in aiming, the aim not being sufficiently exact.

3. Some defect in the sight, such as the left eye being the more powerful, etc.

4. Misfit of gun.

5. Nervousness, occasioning flinching and depression of muzzle at moment of firing.

Of course it is impossible to say which of these faults apply to " E. F. A. Y.," but if he can decide for himself and inform you, Mr. Editor, or your correspondents, I think he would be more likely to get the information and remedy he requires. At the same time he should remember that " Rome was not built in a day," nor was the art of shooting acquired in a like period of time, and that faults once learnt are very difficult to unlearn.

MIDLANDS

Miss Annie Oakley (Little Sure Shot), the cele-brated American Lady Shot, who visited England in 1887 with Buffalo Bill's Wild West Show, writes :—

"NEW YORK, *8th Dec.*, 1888.

"DEAR SIR,—The four breech-loading hammerless guns you built for me are, in my opinion, as near perfection as it is possible to get them. The pair of 20-bores (weight 5 lbs. 2 ozs.), I have been using now nearly two years. I find them just as tight and sound as when new; I have never had any repairs except having the locks cleaned. The pair of 12-bores (6 lbs.) are as good as the 20's.

Since using your guns, and receiving a few lessons from you at your splendid private shooting grounds, my shooting in the field has so much improved that now I always make a good score, even at fast and difficult birds. With many thanks for the pains you have taken in making me such perfect fitting and fine shooting guns.

"I am, gratefully yours,

"(Signed)   ANNIE OAKLEY,

"(Little Sure Shot)."

MISS ANNIE OAKLEY again visited London with Buffalo Bill's Wild West Show in 1892.

Clay Pigeon, Starling and Live Pigeon shooting.

Gun Fitting Rifle and Revolver Shooting.

Charles Lancaster's Private Shooting Grounds, close to Willesden Junction, L. & N. W. Ry., near London (6 miles from Marble Arch).

Try Guns, Moving Targets, Clay Pigeon Shooting, and High Tower for practice at imitation driven shots.

LESSONS

IN THE

ART OF SHOOTING.

CHARLES LANCASTER

Has the honour to inform gentlemen that he personally gives Lessons in Shooting at his **Private Shooting Grounds,** by Appointment.

ALSO EXPERTS ATTEND DAILY.

Instruction in Field or Covert. Terms by arrangement.

Best Blue Rocks, for Matches, per doz.	£1	0	0
Ordinary Pigeons	from 12/- to 15/-

Cartridges, Glass Balls "Clay" Pigeons, &c., at usual advertised prices. All Shooting requisites provided, and a Running Rabbit has recently been added.

Gun Metal Moulds for Casting Pitch Balls, as supplied to "Buffalo Bill's" Wild West Show, 45/- each.

Guns by any maker may be used; also altered, should they require it, to fit perfectly.

C. L.'s Original Adjustable Gun (with specially constructed fittings) can be handled in the shop to demonstrate that the measurements taken by him are correct as to bend, length. and cast-off, thereby showing that the Gun to be supplied will be suited to the purchaser.

Use of Try Gun at Private Grounds, 10/6 ; Cartridges, &c., extra.

Attendance in Shop, Re-fit of Gun, 5/-.

No charge for use of these to Customers ordering new Guns.

CHARLES LANCASTER'S PRIVATE SHOOTING GROUNDS

Are situated at Six Miles from the Marble Arch, on the main road to Harrow, passing Kensal Green, Harlesden, leaving Willesden on the left, and Stonebridge Park *en route.*

Frequent Trains from all parts to Willesden Junction Station (L. & N W. Railway)—1¾ miles from Ground—where cabs may be obtained; and ten minutes' walk from Wembley Hill Station, trains from Marylebone Station, G.C.R. Omnibuses leave Charing Cross at fixed times for Stonebridge Park—ten minutes' walk from Ground. Neasden Station, Metropolitan Railway, about 2½ miles from Ground.

Ground may be engaged for Private Matches, Revolver or Rifle Practice, &o.

SEE TESTIMONIALS.

THE FITTING OF GUNS.

CHARLES LANCASTER

Maintains his unrivalled success as a "coach" and "fitter" of Guns to the special individual requirements of his patrons.

Gentlemen in doubt as to the fit of their Guns are invited to use

CHARLES LANCASTER'S

ADJUSTABLE TRY GUNS

(For description see *Field*, 4th July, 1891).

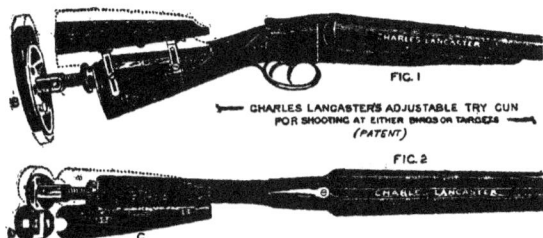

CHARLES LANCASTER'S ADJUSTABLE "TRY GUNS," either with the Ordinary 2 Triggers, or with Patent Single Trigger.

Which can be fired at C. L.'s special fitting Targets, and is constructed with the stock perfectly rigid in the hand, therefore does not give an excess of bend, yet it can be adjusted for cast-off bend and length; also for set of toe or heel of stock, so as to be correctly adjusted to what is required for any individual sportsman to enable him to make accurate practice when firing at either targets or game; or his original Adjustable Gun (with specially constructed fittings) can be handled in the shop to demonstrate that the measurements taken there are correct as to bend, length, and cast-off, thereby showing that the Gun to be supplied will be suited to the purchaser.

GUNS BY OTHER MAKERS ALTERED.

Use of Try Gun at Shooting Grounds, 10/6.

Cartridges, etc., Extra.

ATTENDANCE IN SHOP, RE-FIT OF GUN, 5/-.

No charge for use of these to Customers ordering New Guns.

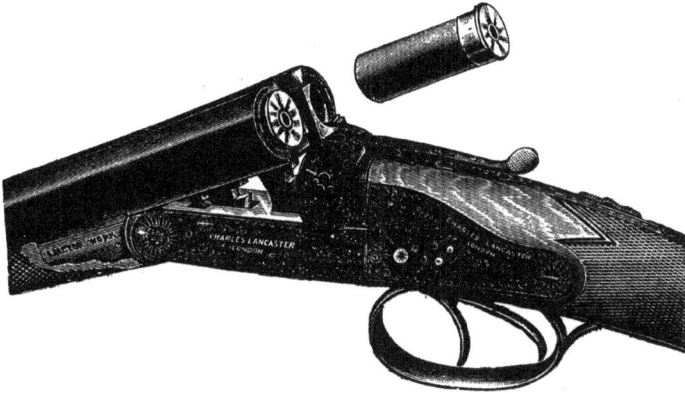

CHARLES LANCASTER'S
GRADE "B" SIDE LOCK
Hammerless Ejector Gun.

£45
EITHER SINGLE OR DOUBLE TRIGGER.
IF WITHOUT EJECTORS, £40.

MANY Customers having expressed their appreciation for Guns with Detachable Side Locks in preference to the well-known Body or Box Action, CHARLES LANCASTER has much pleasure in introducing this **Side Lock Grade "B" Gun**, as illustrated above, to the notice of Sportsmen. It is a thoroughly reliable, well-finished, and high grade Gun.

The Ejector Mechanism consists of his now well tried Two-part Ejector, viz., Mainspring and Ejecting Hammer, described on page 149.

Single Trigger Guns.—In executing orders for above Guns, with Single Trigger, they would be fitted with CHARLES LANCASTER'S Special Mechanism (Patent), modified and approved to date, somewhat similar to that which he introduced in 1895, of which hundreds have been sold and have given satisfaction.

Safety.—All these Guns are fitted with Automatic Trigger, also Intercepting Safety Scears.

Barrels bored either Cylinder, Modified, or "Full Choke."

LATEST TESTIMONIALS.

"Thanks to you for the care and trouble you have taken over the Single Trigger Guns, and I am sure you have fitted me well, and they are a splendid pair of Guns ; also were greatly admired by my friends."—S.

"I was very pleased with the New Gun when trying same at your Shooting Grounds, and shall hope to give it plenty of work."—V.

"The Gun arrived to-day, and I am very pleased with its appearance and finish, and it fits me well."—P.

N.B. CHARLES LANCASTER respectfully informs his patrons that he still continues to supply the Box or Body Action Hammerless Ejector, or Non-Ejector Guns and (as illustrated in Price Lists) to duplicate Guns of that pattern, hundreds of which have been sold, and some of which are always kept in Stock in different stages of manufacture.

CASES AND FITTINGS EXTRA.
The above are Cash Prices.

CHARLES LANCASTER'S
SPECIAL SIDE LOCK
W. & R. HAMMERLESS EJECTOR GUN,
GRADE "C."

£35 NET CASH,
EITHER SINGLE OR DOUBLE TRIGGERS.

For Description of Single-Trigger Mechanism see General Price List.)

IF WITHOUT EJECTOR, £30 NET CASH.

Fitted in Leather Case, with Fittings, **£5** extra.

SPORTSMEN having frequently objected to the designation "Colonial Quality" on a Gun, especially when the Gun has been required mostly for home use, CHARLES LANCASTER has pleasure in bringing this **Grade "C"** Gun to the notice of Sportsmen. It is somewhat similar to his "W. & R. Hammerless Guns" described and illustrated in his General Price List, but of a higher grade. It is fitted with Automatic Trigger, also Intercepting Safety Scears, with Steel Barrels either "Cylinder," "Modified," or "Full Choke."

THESE GUNS ARE CAREFULLY EXAMINED, REGULATED, AND SHOT, AND ARE SUPPLIED IN 12, 16 AND 20 BORES.

THE ABOVE ARE CASH PRICES.

CHARLES LANCASTER'S A. & W.
SPECIAL HAMMERLESS EJECTOR GUN.

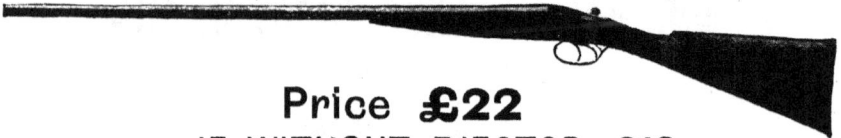

Price £22
IF WITHOUT EJECTOR, £16

IN order to meet the demand for this grade of gun, C. L. has made special arrangements to supply the above (which bears that title only). It is fitted with Automatic Trigger Safety, and Steel Barrels. Also

CHARLES LANCASTER'S W. & R.
HAMMERLESS EJECTOR GUN.

Price £26
IF WITHOUT EJECTOR, £20

THIS gun is of a higher grade than the above (and bears its title only), but is constructed with Side Detachable Locks, and Intercepting Safety Scears. Steel or Damascus Barrels.

All the above Guns are carefully examined, shot, and regulated, and are made in 12, 16 and 20 Bores.

THESE GUNS ARE VERY SUITABLE, ESPECIALLY IN THE SMALLER BORES, FOR PRESENTS TO LADIES AND YOUTHS.

CHARLES LANCASTER, Gunmaker to H.M. the King,
11, PANTON ST., HAYMARKET, LONDON, S.W.
THE ABOVE ARE CASH PRICES.

CHARLES LANCASTER'S
Special Guns for Pigeon Shooting.

WITH HAMMERS,
£30 and £45.

These Guns are specially built for Pigeon Shooting, with Top Lever Snap Action, with Extension Rib, extra strong rebounding Back-action Locks (which do not weaken the action like Guns with Bar Locks). Hammers below the line of sight.

HAMMERLESS EJECTORS,
£50 and £63.

HAMMERLESS,
£40 and £55.

With Automatic or Independent Trigger Safeties and Automatic Blocking Safeties.

These Guns are made with the best English laminated steel barrels, 30 in., bored right "modified choke," left "full choke," chambered for $2\frac{3}{4}$-in. or 3-in. cases. Shooting guaranteed with $3\frac{1}{4}$ drs., $1\frac{1}{4}$ oz. Weight about 7 lbs. 6 ozs. Well finished, with engraving. Instructions for self-measurement sent. Patronized by Members of the Leading Gun Clubs, &c.

If with Whitworth Steel Barrels, £4 extra.

Detailed Price List of Cases for above Guns, also Price of Cartridges, &c., &c., free on application.

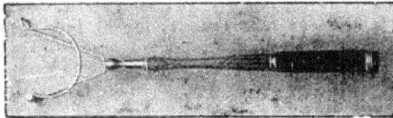

From "THE FIELD," *May 7th, 1898.*

LANCASTER'S "PYGMIES."

Mr. CHARLES LANCASTER has sent a sample of h's "Pygmies" for us to test and report upon. These cartridges are loaded with 28-grs. of Walsrode powder and 1-oz. of No. 6 shot. They were tried in a 12-bore gun with ordinary length of chamber. The velocity given is quite up to our standard of 1160 feet per sec. ; the patterns are good and regular, without the slightest sign of balling, and the pressures are perfectly safe ones.

(Barometer, 29·26-in. ; Thermometer—wet bulb, 60° ; dry, 63°).

12-bore Gun ; weight 7-lb. ; barrels, 30 in. Powder, 28-grs. of Walsrode ; shot, 1-oz. No. 6. (270 pellets). Wadding : thin card, ¾-in. felt, grey cloth, thin card over shot. Gas pressure—average 2·93 tons per sq. in. ; highest round, 3·14 ; lowest, 2·79 tons. Joyce's cases, 2⅛-in. in length ; cartridges, 1¾-in. in length.

RIGHT BARREL.—Forty Yards Pattern.

Round	1st ring	2nd ring	3rd ring	4th ring	5th ring	6th ring	Inside 30-inch Circle	Outside 30 inches	Velocity 10-yards Ft. sec.	Recoil Ft. lb.
1	37	24	22	20	18	16	103	167	1186	22·6
2	30	30	30	21	16	16	111	159	1154	22·1
3	41	28	25	26	14	17	120	150	1128	21·3
4	33	30	28	25	20	12	116	154	1149	20·3
5	36	26	20	16	17	15	98	172	1181	22·4
6	39	31	28	24	20	16	122	148	1158	21·5
7	35	27	24	23	16	13	109	161	1167	21·0
8	42	29	26	22	19	18	119	151	1172	22·0
9	30	24	16	26	22	15	96	174	1141	20·5
10	38	26	25	21	17	14	110	160	1176	22·3
Aver'ge	36	28	24	22	18	15	110	160	1161	21·6

LEFT BARREL.—Forty Yards Pattern.

Round	1st ring	2nd ring	3rd ring	4th ring	5th ring	6th ring	Inside 30-inch Circle	Outside 30 inches	
1	44	55	40	25	12	17	164	106	
2	59	48	37	30	20	15	174	96	
3	68	57	33	24	18	13	182	88	
4	56	50	34	27	15	11	167	103	
5	64	49	36	22	17	13	171	99	Velocity and
6	45	42	30	26	10	21	143	127	Recoil
7	68	46	30	33	16	12	177	93	as above.
8	49	36	24	21	16	20	130	140	
9	51	44	38	29	15	20	162	108	
10	62	57	35	27	19	14	181	89	
Aver'ge	57	48	34	26	16	16	165	105	

The Diameter of the 1st ring is 15 inches ; area 225 circular inches.

"	"	2nd	"	21¼	"	
"	"	3rd	"	26	"	The area of each belt, between
"	"	4th	"	30	"	two rings. is the same as
"	"	5th	"	33¼	"	stated above.
"	"	6th	"	36¼	"	

238

CHARLES LANCASTER,

INVENTOR OF

For Rook, Rabbit, Antelope, Express,

CHARLES LANCASTER'S NON-FOULING SMOOTH OVAL BORE RIFLING

Military and Large Bore Rifles.

Section of barrel rifled on the non-fouling smooth oval-bore system; the dotted lines show the original cylindrical bore (or minor axis) enlarged to an oval (or major axis), thereby making a perfect ellipse.

NON-FOULING SMOOTH OVAL-BORE
MAGNUM
AND
EXPRESS DOUBLE-BARREL B.L. RIFLES,

(·256, ·303, ·360, ·400, ·450, ·500, and ·577).

Cash Prices - - - £36, £45, and £60.

DOUBLE-BARREL B.L. HAMMERLESS RIFLES

Cash £50 and £60.

If fitted with Ejectors, £57 10s. and £70.

SINGLE-BARREL EXPRESS RIFLES,

Cash £16, £18, and £22 10s.

Hammerless, £25 and £35.

LEE-ENFIELD MAGAZINE RIFLES,

·303 Sporting Pattern, from £8 18s. 0d. to £12.

·003 Military Pattern, Government Viewed, from £7 10s. 0d.

SPORTING PATTERN MARTINIS, &c., ALWAYS IN STOCK.

New Sporting Telescopic Sights for all kinds of Rifles in stock.
Testimonials and Price Lists Free.

CHARLES LANCASTER'S

CELEBRATED NON-FOULING
SMOOTH OVAL-BORE
ROOK AND RABBIT RIFLES,

·250, ·300, ·360 and ·380 Bores.

All these are rifled with the **Non-Fouling Smooth Oval-Bore Rifling,** which gives great velocity and flat trajectory, and is the only kind of Rifling that does not foul and that can be cleaned as easily as a Gun Barrel. Shot Cartridges can be used from these Rifles, thereby making them specially suited for Collectors.

No. 1—Under lever snap-action, rebounding lock, ejector. Rook Rifle, straight stock, plain finish. Cash, £5. If with pistol hand stock extra, 10s. nett.

No. 2—Martini-action, B.L. Rook Rifle, with safety; engraved, &c., &c. Cash, £8.

No. 2a-If with plain straight stock. Cash, £5.

No. 3—Under lever snap action, B.L. Rook Rifle; better quality and higher finish, with pistol hand stock. Cash, £8.

No. 4—Best quality and finish, highly engraved, top-lever snap-action B.L. Rook Rifle, with rebounding lock and cartridge ejector Cash, £10.

No. 5—C. L.'s New Hammerless R ok Rifle, side lock. Cash, £12.

Double Barrel Rook and Rabbit Rifles to order.

Orthoptic (or peep) sights fitted to order.

~~~~~~~~~~~~~

ELEY'S AND KYNOCH'S CARTRIDGES ARE USED,

WHICH CAN BE OBTAINED ANYWHERE.

		£	s.	d.
Brown or Black Canvas Cases, with divisions for Cartridges	from nett	1	10	0
Brown or Black Canvas Cases, for Martini-action Rifles	,,	1	15	0
Solid Leather Cases	,,	2	12	0
Solid Leather Cases, for Martini-action Rifles	,,	3	0	0
Plain Deal Packing Cases for Rifle only	,,	0	2	6
Recapping Tools, &c., per set	,,	0	18	0
Brass Cleaning Rods	,,	0	4	6
Steel do. do. in three pieces	,,	0	7	6
Iron Cleaning Rod	,,	0	3	0
Turnscrew	,,	0	2	0
Nickel Plated Sight Protector	,,	0	3	6
Waterproof Covers, to take Rifle full length	from nett 5s. to	0	12	6
Conical Bullet Mould (to cast solid or shell)	from nett	0	15	0
Spherical Bullet Mould	,,	0	5	0
Strong Iron Target, 15 by 14 in., with ringing Bull's-eye, 2 in.	,,	2	2	0
Card Targets, 9¼ in. square, with 1½ in. Bull's-eye	per doz. ,,	0	1	0

The perfect shooting of these Rifles is guaranteed ; if not approved of may be exchanged. They can be tested, before purchase, at Lancaster's Shooting Grounds near Willesden Junction, L. & N. W. Railway.

CHARLES LANCASTER

Begs most respectfully to draw the attention of Sportsmen to his

BALL AND SHOT GUN
"THE COLINDIAN."

(TRADE MARK REGISTERED.)

FOR "CORDITE" OR BLACK POWDER.

A non-fouling smooth oval-bore Rifled Gun, shooting elongated conical-shaped Bullets accurately from 20 to 100 yards, and shot of all sizes, as well as a Gun, and which has neither grooved rifling nor choke boring to offer resistance to shot or ball, and consequently prevents leading, fouling, and undue recoil.

These guns are accurately sighted at 50 and 100 yards. Loads—3drs. of powder and "Express" bullet 765 grs. (1¾oz.), 4 drs. of powder and "Express" bullet with steel plug. The Guns have been largely used with most satisfactory results both at big game and feather, in Europe, Asia, Africa and America.

As supplied to H.I.M.'s Government of India and many well-known Sportsmen in all parts of the world.

PRICES.

Top Lever Snap-Action Double-Barrel B.L. Hammer Gun, with Rebounding Locks, Hammers below the line of sight.

£27, £36, and £45.

Top Lever Snap-Action Double-barrel B.L. Hammerless Gun, with Automatic Trigger Safety and Blocking Safeties, easily taken to pieces for cleaning. Highly praised for its strength and simple action by the Editor of "The Field," &c., &c.

£36, £45, and £50.

These Guns are 12, 16 and 20 bore, and chambered for Eley's ordinary central-fire Cases, and are about 7¼ lbs. weight.

Hammerless Ejector, £44, £55, and £63.

These Guns may be tested at C.L.'s Private Range before purchase.

A sportsman having one of the above Guns, and a "Double-barrel Express Rifle," is fully equipped for Sport in any part of the World.

PRICES FOR CASES, IMPLEMENTS, &c., &c.

	CASH.
Solid Leather Cases	£3 0 0
Mail Canvas Case, best quality Spring Lock	1 15 0
"Colonial Quality" Set of Implements complete	1 5 0
Best Quality Solid Leather Pigeon Bat Gun Case, with Patent Lever Lock, and fitted for Cleaning Rod and Turnscrew	3 3 0
Second Quality ditto	2 2 0
Mail Canvas ditto	2 5 0
Ditto, Plain Lock ditto	1 5 0
Mail Canvas Waterproof Gun Cover	0 13 6
„ „ with Sling	1 1 0
Twilled Waterproof Gun Cover, Lined	0 15 0
Check „ „	0 7 6
*Mould and Core Pegs	1 5 0
*Compressor for fixing Bullets in Cartridge Cases	0 7 6
*Combination Brass Powder and Shot Measure	0 4 6
Cleaning Rod with apparatus .. .. from	0 10 6
„	0 6 6
„	0 5 0
*Wooden Rammer	0 1 0
Turnscrews .. .. each	0 2 6
Loaded Cartridges, Solid or "Express" Bullets .. .. per 100	1 7 0
Loaded with Shot (See Cartridge List).	
Bullets, Solid or "Express" .. .. .. per 100	0 12 6
Steel Plugs for "Express" Bullets .. .. from per doz.	0 2 0
Eley's Cartridge Cases, 12-bore, green .. .. per 100	0 4 0
Felt Wads .. .. per lb.	0 3 0
Card „ .. .. per 1,000	0 0 6

TIN-LINED PACKING CASES EXTRA.

* These Implements should be ordered with "The Colindian."

R

SPORT WITH THE COLINDIAN (REG'D)

(PRICE FROM 27£)

A SPECIALITY
NON-FOULING
SMOOTH OVAL BORE

TIGER

S.G. SHOT

DUCK & GEESE

C.L's MEDIUM GAME SHOT
FOR PHEASANTS & HARES

ELEPHANT

BALL & SHOT GUN

WITHOUT CHOKE BORING OR GROOVED RIFLING THEREBY PREVENTING LEADING
AND UNDUE RECOIL SHOOTING FROM BOTH BARRELS SHOT OF ALL SIZES
AS WELL AS A GUN. & HOLLOW POINTED SOLID OR STEEL TIPPED CONNICAL
BULLETS ACCURATLY TO 100 YARDS   CHAS LANCASTER

COPYRIGHT

DEER & WILD BOAR

PARTRIDGE & SNIPE

6 & 8 SHOT

THE
"LANCASTER GLOAMING SIGHT."

An Enamelled Tipped Sheath Foresight.

From " The Field," 18th March, 1893.

There are times when shooting with a Sporting Rifle takes place under difficulties, and amongst others which must be contended with may be ranked

A FAILING LIGHT AND A GLARING LIGHT.

In either of these cases

THE ORDINARY RIFLE SIGHT IS OF NO ASSISTANCE;

So with the object of rendering some aid to the shooter, Mr. CHARLES LANCASTER, of 11, Panton Street, Haymarket, has designed this sheath sight, which, as the accompanying illustration shows,

is of tubular form, with a white enamel circular face at one extremity.

The sight has a spring clip, which enables anyone to slide it on to the ordinary front sight.

THE SHOOTER HAS THEN A WHITE ENAMEL GUIDE FOR HIS AIM
WHICH WILL HELP HIM WHEN LIGHT IS VANISHING,
OR WHEN THE SUN SHINES WITH EXCESSIVE BRILLIANCY.

On reference to the engraving it will be seen that the circles of the " Gloaming " sights are of various diameters, so that individual tastes and differing circumstances can be provided for.

PRICE—

Set of four, in case ... ... 14s.
Single Sight ... ... 3s. 6d. each.

CHARLES LANCASTER,
Gun & Rifle Manufacturer,
11, PANTON STREET, HAYMARKET, LONDON, S.W.
N.B.—The Trade Supplied.

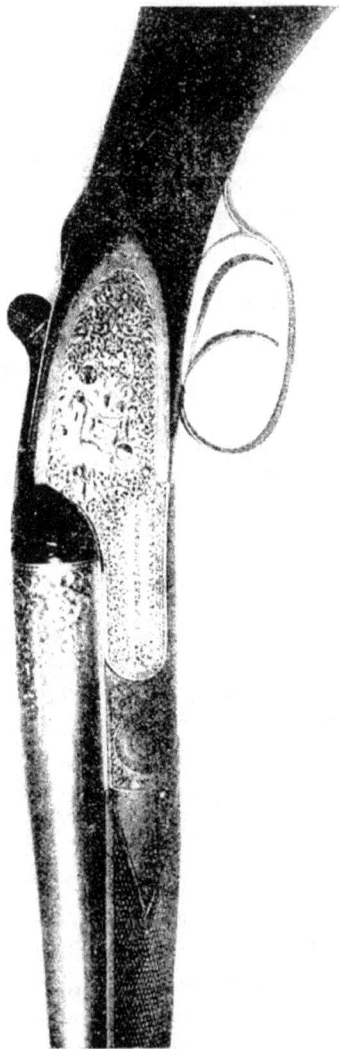

The "Ross" Straight-pull Magazine Sporting Rifle

(PATENT)

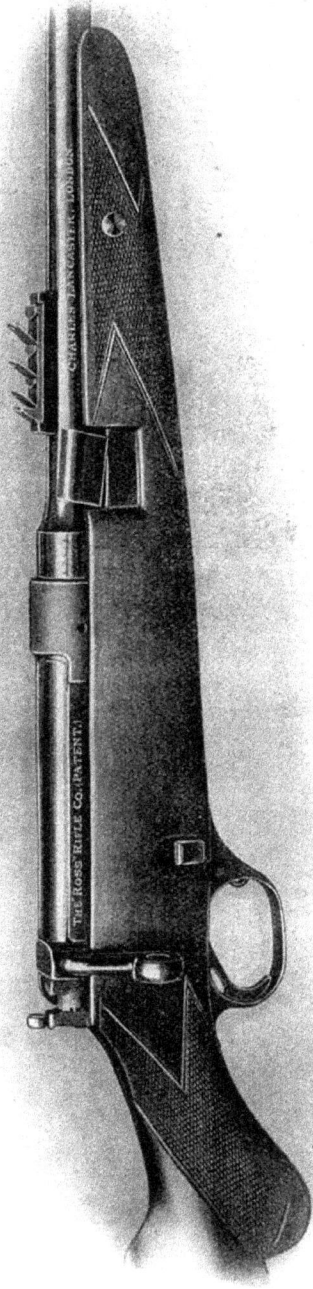

FOR DEER STALKING AND BIG GAME SHOOTING.

Supplied in ·256 and ·303 at £15 and £20, and ·370 at £20 and £25.

CASE AND FITTINGS EXTRA.

Full Particulars of— **CHARLES LANCASTER.**

" Getting ready for Covert Shooting."

CHARLES LANCASTER'S SHOOTING GROUNDS.

CHARLES LANCASTER'S

A. & M.

PARCELS POST

Folding Cases for Game,

WITH TAPES, &c.

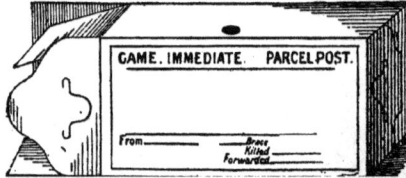

These are packed and stored FLAT, *and so occupy little space.*
Great economy of room in storing.

	Inches.	Covered Brown Paper.		Covered Calico.	
		Per Gross. Per Doz.		Per Gross. Per Doz.	
1 Brace Partridges,	$3\frac{3}{4} \times 3\frac{3}{4} \times 10$	... 25/-	... 2/3 ...	40/-	... 3/6
2 " "	$7\frac{1}{2} \times 3\frac{3}{4} \times 10$	... 31/6	... 2/10 ...	50/6	... 4/6
3 " "	$8 \times 4 \times 14$	... 36/-	... 3/4 ...	61/0	... 5/3
4 " "	... ...	... ...	... 4/6	... ...	... 5/9
1 Brace Pheasants,	$10 \times 7\frac{1}{2} \times 3\frac{3}{4}$	... 31/6	... 2/10 ...	50/6	... 4/6
2 " "	$10\frac{1}{2} \times 4 \times 15$	... 49/-	... 4/4 ...	69/-	... 6/-
3 " "	$10\frac{1}{2} \times 5\frac{3}{4} \times 15$	... 99/-	... 8/4 ...	144/-	... 12/-
1 Brace Grouse ...	$8 \times 4 \times 8$	... 29/-	... 2/6 ...	47/6	... 4/-
2 " "	$8 \times 4 \times 14$	... 36/-	... 3/- ...	61/-	... 5/2
3 " "	$10\frac{1}{2} \times 4 \times 15$	... 49/-	... 4/2 ...	69/-	... 5/9

QUOTATIONS FOR WOODEN BOXES ON APPLICATION.

ALSO

Non-collapsible Game Boxes for 1, 2, 3 & 4 Brace.

PRICES ON APPLICATION.

11, PANTON STREET, HAYMARKET,

LONDON, S.W.

Registered Telegraphic Address—
"OVAL BORE LONDON."

Telephone No.—
3691 GERARD.

THE "LANCASTER" SMOCK,

MADE IN

Burberry's Celebrated Gabardine Combinations.

BURBERRY, BASINGSTOKE.

London Show Rooms:—30, HAYMARKET, S.W.

Extract from "FIELD" *of Nov. 28th, 1891, p. 808.*

"I have now a garment which will keep out the heaviest of rains, even if driven by a gale; and at the same time I am able to get a 'right and left' either from a 'butt, field of roots, or covert side, without let or hindrance. I feel sure that many will welcome this useful addition to their sporting kit, as I consider it just as useful to a yachtsman or an angler as to a 'gunner.' The material is perfectly waterproof, yet not in the least air-proof, as you can both breathe and smoke through it; and the Smock does not cause perspiration, as, being cut 'full,' plenty of room is given for ventilation.

"CHARLES LANCASTER."

PRICES FROM 42/- TO 63/- NETT.

Measurements required — Height; Size round chest over ordinary shooting coat; Length from collar of coat to just below the knee.

——:o:——

Orders to CHARLES LANCASTER, 11, Panton St., Haymarket, S.W.

The Keepers' Benefit Society.

FOUNDED 1886.

Patron—H.R.H. THE PRINCE OF WALES.

PRESIDENT.

THE DUKE OF PORTLAND.

COMMITTEE.

═ RULES ═

1.—The object of this Society is to provide for the widows or families of Keepers who lose their lives by violence in the protection of game, deer, or fish ; also to provide with a yearly income those Keepers who can produce a certificate from their present or late Master, countersigned by a Justice of the Peace and a duly qualified Medical Practitioner, appointed by the Committee, that they are totally and permanently incapacitated from contributing in any way to their own maintenance on account of old age or accident. Such certificates must be renewed every six months. The word " Keeper " shall mean any person who is wholly employed in the protection of game, deer, or fish for sporting purposes. No Keeper can be admitted to the benefits of the Society unless he has been two years in his present or three years in his last situation, and who is in receipt of less than 12s. per week.

2.—Widows or families who come under the description given in Rule 1 will be entitled to receive £75 in a lump sum. After providing for these widows and families, and also for working expenses, the income of the Society shall be divided annually in equal sums, not exceeding £25, among those Benefit Members who are totally and permanently incapacitated from contributing in any way to their own maintenance on account of old age or accident. No Benefit Member under 60 shall be considered to be incapacitated on account of old age.

3.—Honorary Members shall pay a minimum Yearly Subscription of 2 Guineas (due 1st January), or a Life Subscription of 25 Guineas. Donations of smaller sums will be received.

N.B.—CHARLES LANCASTER is a Life Member.

4.—No Keeper over the age of 50 shall be allowed to join the Society. All Subscriptions of Benefit Members shall be paid for the whole of life, whether the Member be in receipt of annuity *or not.*

5.—A Committee for the year, to include at least two Benefit Members, shall be appointed at the Annual General Meeting.

6.—The Committee shall have it in their power to expel any Benefit Member from the Society who has been proved to their satisfaction to have been guilty of any gross misconduct; such Member to forfeit any money that he has paid, and to have no further claim on the Society.

7.—Any Benefit Member who is One year in arrear of his Subscription shall, at the discretion of the Committee, forfeit any money that he has paid, and shall cease to be a Member of the Society. He may, however, at the discretion of the Committee, be re-admitted within five years on payment of arrears. No Benefit Member who has ceased to be a Keeper, and who has adopted some other occupation, shall continue to belong to the Society, unless he shall have been a Member for ten years. This rule is not intended to apply to Benefit Members who may be out of a Keeper's place for any period not exceeding two years.

8.—The Secretary of the Society shall pay the allowances to the Benefit Members, and receive all Subscriptions.

9.—All disputes and questions whatsoever, and particularly questions as to persons who may be provided for under Rule 1, and questions as to what portion of the annual receipts of the Society shall be considered as income, and what portion shall be accumulated or otherwise dealt with, shall be decided by the Committee in their absolute discretion, and their decision shall be final.

10.—The Committee shall have power to add to their number, and to alter any existing Rule, and also to make any additional Rules that they may think requisite.

11.—There shall be a General Meeting of the Society held every year, in London on the Friday before Ascot.

12.—A list of Benefit Members requiring situations to be kept at the Office of the Society.

13.—An Actuarial Examination of the affairs of the Society shall be made every five years.

14.—The Annual Subscriptions of Benefit Members are due 1st July. Those joining between January 1st and June 30th shall not pay another premium until July 1st in the year following.

The following is the Scale of Annual Subscriptions for Benefit Members:—

Age.			Annual Subscriptions.				Age			Annual Subscriptions.		
Under 30	..	..	..	£0	15	0	Under 41	..	..	.. £2	7	0
„ 31	..	..	..	0	16	0	„ 42	..	..	.. 2	12	0
„ 32	..	..	..	0	18	0	„ 43	..	..	.. 2	17	0
„ 33	..	..	..	1	0	0	„ 44	..	..	.. 3	2	0
„ 34	..	..	..	1	2	0	„ 45	..	..	.. 3	8	0
„ 35	..	..	..	1	5	0	„ 46	..	..	.. 3	14	0
„ 36	..	..	..	1	8	0	„ 47	..	..	.. 4	0	0
„ 37	..	..	..	1	11	0	„ 48	..	..	.. 4	6	0
„ 38	..	..	..	1	15	0	„ 49	..	..	.. 4	13	0
„ 39	..	..	..	1	19	0	„ 50	..	..	.. 5	0	0
„ 40	..	..	..	2	3	0						

The sum paid by the Society to Pensioners is over £8,400.

The Field Sports Protection and Encouragement Association.

THIS Association was formed in 1884 as THE NATIONAL SPORTS PROTECTION AND DEFENCE ASSOCIATION, and it was found at the first Annual General Meeting held in 1885, that its organisation (a work of considerable labour) was good ; it was considered that it might still serve the true interests of Sports and Sportsmen, and the public had liberally responded. It was then decided to change its title to THE FIELD SPORTS PROTECTION AND ENCOURAGEMENT ASSOCIATION, which, as its name denotes, is intended to protect and encourage the Sports of Hunting, Racing, Shooting, Fishing, and Coursing ; and to render assistance in opposing attacks on such Sports, to watch all legislative and other proposals likely to affect them adversely, and to raise funds necessary for such purposes.

There not being any combination of the various Sporting interests in existence previous to the formation of this Society to take the initiative on occasions arising, and as the encouragement of Field Sports is of importance to the public, the Executive Council trusts the Association will meet with the support of the public, who, in subscribing, have the guarantee of a most responsible body of leading Sportsmen, that the funds will be distributed in a manner worthy of their confidence, and, of late, much work has been done, and a considerable sum of money expended in upholding the interests of sport.

Annual Subscription, £1 ; a Donation of £5 and upwards constitutes Life Membership.

On application to the Secretary, further particulars will be sent illustrating the value of the Association to Sportsmen.

THE
Abbey Improved Chilled Shot Company, Ltd.

D	12	11	10	9
2600 per oz.	1250 per oz.	1040 per oz.	850 per oz.	580 per oz.
8	**7**	**6½**	**6**	**5½**
450 per oz.	340 per oz.	300 per oz.	270 per oz.	240 per oz.
5	**4**	**3**	**2**	**1**
218 per oz.	172 per oz.	140 per oz.	122 per oz.	104 per oz.
B	**2/B**	**3/B**	**A**	**2/A**
98 per oz.	84 per oz.	66 per oz.	56 per oz.	48 per oz.
3/A	**SSSG**	**SSG**	**SG**	**LG**
40 per oz.	15 per oz.	11 per oz.	8½ per oz.	6 per ox.

SOLE MANUFACTURERS OF IMPROVED CHILLED SHOT, AND
MAKERS OF HARD AND PATENT SHOT.
NEWCASTLE-ON-TYNE.
Samples sent on application. Before Buying Elsewhere send for our Prices.
SPORTSMEN SPEAK HIGHLY OF "I. C." SHOT.

BURBERRY

HINTS TO GUNNERS.

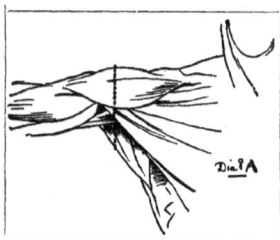

Diag. A

DIFFICULT SHOTS.—Experts differ in regard to the shot that presents the greatest difficulty, but the most difficult shot is comparatively easy when arms and shoulders have perfect liberty, a fact realised by anyone wearing a coat fitted with **Burberry Patent Pivot Sleeves.** The advantages of these sleeves our diagrams indicate, and a practical test convincingly proves. Your tailor "trusses up" the most important muscles by a seam round them (*see dotted line diagram A*), that forms an inflexible band which, when arm is raised and muscles stretched to fullest extent, cuts into them like a knife.

The BURBERRY PIVOT SLEEVE has no traverse binding seam; the seams follow lines of muscles (see diagram D), and go with their every movement, so that even in difficult shots you score "kills" not "misses."

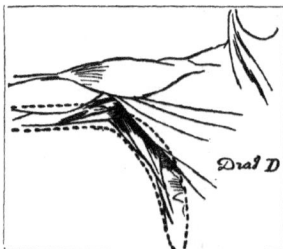

Diag. D

BURBERRYS put **PIVOT SLEEVES** into all shooting coats, and perfect liberty of movement results.

See following pages.

BURBERRYS, HAYMARKET, LONDON, and BASINGSTOKE.

BURBERRY

HINTS TO GUNNERS.

THE BURBERRY PIVOT SLEEVE.
(PATENT.)

Pronounced perfect by Shooting, Golfing and Fishing Experts.

AVOIDS that customary feeling of TIGHTNESS under the ARMPITS.

The BODY OF the COAT WON'T LIFT when both arms are held straight up.

Gets AHEAD of all other schemes for LIBERATING ARMS AND SHOULDERS.

Improves shooting twenty-five per cent.

" *The coat had plenty of useful pockets and really wonderful pivot sleeves, which allow absolute freedom of arm movement in every direction without the least drag being felt—a perfect sleeve for golfing and shooting.*"—COUNTRY LIFE.

" *I found, when swinging, a freedom which I have never before experienced in any other coat.*"—" NIBLICK."—ILLUSTRATED SPORTING AND DRAMATIC NEWS.

" *The trial rendered it simply ridiculous to think of shooting fishing, or playing golf in any other garment.*" — BADMINTON MAGAZINE.

BURBERRYS, HAYMARKET, LONDON, and BASINGSTOKE,

BURBERRY
SLIP-ON.

Ample in cut, shields wearer from collar to gaiters, and permits absolute freedom for quick movement. Extremely light, its resistance to rain is unequalled by anything short of oilskins, yet it is healthfully self-ventilating. After years of world-wide trial in storm and flood, the SLIP-ON holds the field, the Sportsman's best over-garment extant. The Press, the Medical Profession and Sportsmen are unanimous in its praise.

> *"Efficient in heaviest rains, healthful in all weathers, light, portable & practical."*
> Country Life.
>
> *Smoke may be blown through the cloth.*

> *"Rain runs off it like dew from a leaf."*
> Lancet.
>
> *"Keeps the wearer dry under heavy rains."*
> Times.

The SLIP-ON'S characteristics may be summarised as follows :—

WEATHERPROOF—Does not admit nor soak up rain.

SELF - VENTILATING—Healthful, and free from unnatural heat.

WEIGHTLESS—Does not tire its owner through day's hard rain.

SHELTERING—Excludes cold wind and dust as well as rain.

UNHAMPERING—The one overcoat with perfect liberty for accurate shooting.

> *Two Articles of interest to the Gunner . .*
> **"BURBERRY-WEAVE-PROOFS."**
> **"DIFFICULT SHOTS,"** see previous pages.

BURBERRYS, HAYMARKET, LONDON, and BASINGSTOKE.

E.C. N⁰·3

TRADE   MARK.

SMOKELESS SPORTING POWDER.

The E. C. Powder Co., Ltd., rank before all other manufacturers in respect of the two most important advances made during the last quarter of a century in sporting explosives, they having introduced hard grain nitro-powders in the first place, and latterly having originated smokeless sporting powder of the so-called 33-grain type.

E. C. POWDER is truly smokeless, and produces no blow-back, its ignition is very quick, its combustion of such regularity that perfect results may always be relied upon, its recoil is reduced to a minimum, and its heating effect upon the gun is practically negligible.

E. C. POWDER is the most adaptable sporting powder known; it may be used in all bores of sporting guns from 4-bore to ·410, and with every bore various loads may be used according to the desire of the sportsman to obtain high, low, or medium velocity, open or concentrated patterns, or extra light recoil should there be a tendency to gun headache.

E. C. POWDER may be relied upon in all temperatures and climates, and may be stored for indefinite periods without alteration or deterioration.

E. C. POWDER does not corrode gun-barrels; but, on the other hand, during its combustion it evolves a material which actually serves as a protection against rusting.

The public is cautioned against the use of poor imitations of E. C. No. 3, with high-sounding names, and also (especially abroad) of powders coloured to resemble E. C., and fraudulently sold as being the genuine article.

THE "E. C." POWDER COMPANY, LTD.,

40, NEW BROAD STREET, LONDON, E.C.

Books Published at the "Field" Newspaper Office.

"MODERN DOGS OF GREAT BRITAIN AND IRELAND."

Sporting Division in Two Vols. Third and Entirely New Edition.

By RAWDON B. LEE.

Illustrated by ARTHUR WARDLE.

Price **21/-** net.

"HANDY GUIDE to the GAME LAWS,"

With Abridgments of the Acts relating to Game.

By a SOLICITOR.

Price **2/6** net.

"FOXES AT HOME, AND . . REMINISCENCES."

By COLONEL J. S. TALBOT.

(Illustrated.)

Price **5/-** net.

"GAME AND FOXES."

By F. W. MILLARD.

Price **3/6**

"FIELD" OFFICE, Windsor House, Breams Buildings, E.C.

SPORTSMEN

Purchasing new Guns can dispose of their old ones at very good prices by advertising them for sale in the columns of "THE BAZAAR, EXCHANGE AND MART" Newspaper, which is the only paper devoted to the purchase or the disposal of private property by Private Persons.

"Like all grand conceptions the process is remarkable for its simplicity."—Globe.

In addition to the special facilities that "THE BAZAAR EXCHANGE AND MART" Newspaper offers for the purchase or disposal of Private Property, the journal contains practical illustrated articles on Fishing, Gardening, Cycling, The Keeping of Farm Stock, Dogs, Poultry, Pigeons, and other subjects interesting to Sportsmen, and all who delight in country pursuits. Established 38 years.

Get a copy and see for yourself. The Paper, which is well worth careful perusal, is to be obtained at all Newsagents and Railway Bookstalls. Price, 2d., or direct from the Office, for 3 penny stamps.

Bazaar Buildings, Drury Lane, London, W.C.

BOOKS FOR SPORTSMEN.

Illustrated Sporting Books.—And their values. Dealing with English Illustrated Works of a Sporting and Racy Character, and Prints relating to Sports of the Field. A very valuable book to all Owners or Collectors of old Sporting Books or Prints. By J. H. SLATER. *In cloth gilt, price 5/-, by post 5/4.*

Practical Game Preserving.—Containing the fullest Directions for Rearing and Preserving both Winged and Ground Game, and Destroying Vermin; with other Information of Value to the Game Preserver. By W. CARNEGIE. New Edition, thoroughly revised, and with much new matter and special plates of different species of Pheasants, the English and Red-legged Partridge, the Stoat, Weasel and Polecat, by Frohart. Plates of other Pheasants used for crossing and many other illustrations. *In cloth gilt, price 7/6, by post, 8/-.*

Practical Sea Fishing.—A Comprehensive Handbook for Amateurs and others on the best tackle and the most successful methods to be pursued for the capture of the different fish around our coasts. The most complete book on the subject yet issued. By P. L. HASLOPE. Copiously illustrated. *In cloth gilt, price 3/6, by post 3/9.*

Breaking and Training Dogs.—Being Concise Directions for the proper education of Dogs, both for the Field and for Companions. Second Edition. By "PATHFINDER." With Chapters by HUGH DALZIEL. Illustrated. *In cloth gilt, price 6s. 6d., by post 6s. 10d.*

Practical Trapping.—Being some Papers on Traps and Trapping for Vermin, with a Chapter on General Bird Trapping and Snaring. By W. CARNEGIE. *Price 1s., by post 1s. 2d.*

Ferrets and Ferreting.—Containing Instructions for the Breeding, Management, and Working of Ferrets. Second Edition, Re-written and greatly Enlarged. Illustrated. *Price 6d., by post 7d.*

London: L. UPCOTT GILL, Bazaar Buildings, Drury Lane, London, W.C.

Season 1906.

KYNOCH

NEW POWDER.

———❦———

No Unconsumed Particles.

No Blow-back.

Absolutely Smokeless.

Light Recoil with Standard Charges.

No Fouling.

33 GRAINS OF SAME SPACE OF BLACK  **OCCUPY THE AS 3 DRAMS POWDER.**

———◉———

Loaded in " Primax," " Kynoid," " Opex " Cartridges.

F. RISDON

(From FAGG BROTHERS),

128, JERMYN STREET, HAYMARKET, LONDON, S.W.

Waterproof Leather for Boots and Gaiters.

NO RUBBER USED.

Always Pliable and Waterproof as long as the Leather is sound.

Shooting Boots	... ...	**40/-**
Alpine Boots	... ...	**42/-**

AN IDEAL PAPER FOR SPORTSMEN!

THE

SHOOTING TIMES.

Bright! Instructive! Readable!

Deals Thoroughly with Three Subjects.

SHOOTING,

**Experts in
all Departments.** FISHING,

DOGS.

Price 10s. 10d. per year, or 2d. weekly.

IF YOU WANT A GUN!

IF YOU WANT A SHOOT!

IF YOU WANT A DOG!

IF YOU WANT A KEEPER!

IF YOU WANT **ANYTHING**

In the Shooting World Advertise in the Miscellaneous Columns of

THE SHOOTING TIMES.

If you have a Dog or a Gun, or anything for Sale, you will not
find a better or cheaper medium.

*Small "Wanted" Advertisements, 18 words 6d. 1d. for each additional
3 words.*

Offices : 72 to 76, TEMPLE CHAMBERS, BOUVERIE ST., FLEET ST.,

LONDON, E.C.

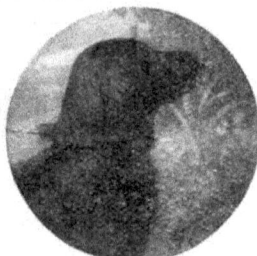

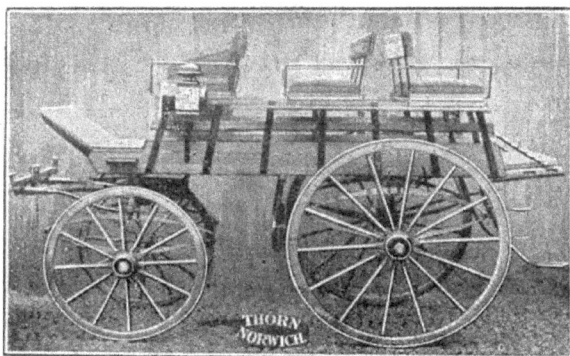